DISCOURSE: A CRITIQUE AND SYNTHESIS OF MAJOR THEORIES

TIMOTHY W. CRUSIUS

D0827147

T 10289

THE MODERN LANGUAGE ASSOCIATION OF AMERICA
NEW YORK, NY   1989

Library of Congress Cataloging-in-Publication Data

Crusius, Timothy W., 1950–
   Discourse : a critique and synthesis of major theories / Timothy W. Crusius.
     p.   cm.
   Includes bibliographical references
   ISBN 0–87352–189–7   ISBN 0–87352–190–0 (pbk.)
   1. Discourse analysis. 2. Rhetoric. I. Title
P302.C75   1989
808'.0014—dc20   89–14571

Published by The Modern Language Association of America
10 Astor Place, New York, New York 10003-6981

To my wife,
ELIZABETH,
and our son,
MICAH

ACKNOWLEDGMENTS

I wish to thank my department head, Hamlin Hill, for course release
time at a crucial juncture in the preparation of this book; my dean,
Daniel Fallon, for funds that supported its final typing; and Liza McVity,
whose compensation for typing was not commensurate with her efforts.
I would also like to acknowledge the work of Stephen M. North and
Richard W. Bailey, who gave the manuscript very helpful readings.

CONTENTS

INTRODUCTION

Caught up ourselves in the revival of rhetoric in English departments over the last quarter-century, we may lack the historical distance to assess its meaning and value. We can say, however, that composition differs markedly now from what it was, whether in the more immediate or the more distant past. Among true professionals composition is no longer simply "theme writing," as it was when I took that freshman course only twenty years ago, faithfully grinding out short essays addressed to no one and about nothing meaningful. While, of course, stubborn pockets of resistance are still holding out, the old freshman English course has become an anachronism.

Composition is no longer what it was for the ancient world—the art of persuasion. Perhaps we long at times for the old oral world of rhetoric, whose very life was face-to-face contention, whose art had not receded in the face of the printed and computer-processed word and a host of other cultural developments. Insofar as the values of the old oral economy survive at all, they survive in speech, and not in our text-centered English departments.

For us, rhetoric is the art of written discourse—all of it, from the predominantly informative and persuasive discourse in our general composition program, to the technical and business communication in our more specialized courses. Although some kinds of writing, for example, journalism, have migrated to other departments, we still think of rhetoric as the entire field of written discourse, a perspective that has no parallel in the history of our discipline.

The slow turn of rhetoric from the oral to the written can be traced through developments in what Walter Ong calls "technologies of the word" (*Presence* 22–92). Also in the psychocultural history of the word lie the clues for understanding our expansive view of rhetoric. However we account for it, we must grant that four specific theories have helped us to envision the universe of discourse.

The first to appear was James Moffett's *Teaching the Universe of Discourse.* Inspired by and inspiring the language arts movement, this book has had enormous impact, especially, but not exclusively, below the college level.

James Kinneavy's *Theory of Discourse* came next. In marked contrast to Moffett, Kinneavy is rooted in traditional literary studies and in classical rhetoric, languages, and philosophy. Reflecting an encyclopedic knowledge of the liberal arts tradition, *Theory*'s appeal does not yet reach significantly beyond the university level.

The Development of Writing Abilities (11–18), by James Britton et al., differs from the others on a number of counts. The book was written by a team of researchers in England. It is not primarily theory but a lengthy empirical study of student writing. While theory occupies only a few chapters, it has a special authority backed by analysis of thousands of student manuscripts. Again, unlike the others, what we shall call Britton's theory (though neither solely theory nor solely Britton's) is explicitly not intended for the classroom.

No less distinctive is Frank D'Angelo's *Conceptual Theory of Rhetoric.* Instead of presenting discourse typologies, D'Angelo concentrates on developing a contemporary understanding of the traditional divisions of rhetoric—invention, arrangement, and style—which he sees as the application of a topical system at various levels and phases of composing. He is the only one of our theorists to embrace wholeheartedly the prospect of a *science* of rhetoric.

From minimal description, one can sense the diversity of these theories. Superficially, they seem to have little in common; apart from Britton's use of Moffett, they do not borrow noticeably from one another. Even their attitudes toward theory itself diverge. For Moffett, theory has value only as it helps to establish learning sequences and teaching attitudes and strategies; he is diffident about theory, almost apologetic, saying at one point that his concept spinning is "essentially an illusion." Compared with Moffett, Kinneavy is aggressively theoretical: for him, theory must articulate, structure, and justify the field of English, within which the study and teaching of discourse have their place.

For Britton, theory is simply necessary to interpret what would otherwise be nothing more than thousands of student scripts: here theory must guide research. For D'Angelo, theory means scientific theory: he wants to supplement the traditional view of rhetoric as an art with rhetoric as a science, grounding the whole in psychology, in a theory of mind.

Part 1 attempts to do justice to each theory as a unique thought structure. The purpose is to analyze and evaluate; the method is a combination of reflection on each theory in itself and comparative assessment. Part 2 turns from analysis to synthesis, offering a single theory incorporating the best of all four.

The field of written composition scarcely suffers from lack of theoretical effort. But compared, for example, with the theoretical outpouring in literary studies over the past decade, our efforts have been somewhat intermittent and disjointed. Before the publication of Walter Beale's *Pragmatic Theory of Rhetoric* in 1987, the last comprehensive, book-length theoretical statement by an English department rhetorician had been D'Angelo's, more than ten years before. Less ambitious contributions certainly appeared in the interim, but large-scale engagement suffered a lapse of about eleven years. Moreover, during the same interval, surprisingly little was written about the influential theories that will concern us here—no more, it is shocking to say, than reviews, a handful of essays, and scattered commentary. The theories were certainly discussed and used (at conferences and in textbooks, for instance), but not carefully assessed in a concentrated way. This study attempts such an assessment in the hope of opening a too-long-neglected argument, one going on, to be sure, even engaged in passionately by a few, but not going on where it should be—at the center of our discipline.

This book speaks to the theories, rather than the theorists (all of whom have written much, barely mentioned here, both before and after their major theoretical books). But it cannot engage, except occasionally in passing, the much larger domain of discourse study and rhetorical theory, either within the field of composition or outside it—in speech, pragmatics, language philosophy, and literary criticism. The intense focus of this book is indispensable to its mission. The focus is a necessity. It does not arise from a desire to exclude or dismiss any source of insight into discourse or rhetoric. It should not even be taken as implying that I think these four theories are necessarily the best available. In our field, however, they have been and are still the most influential, playing major roles in conceiving writing programs, course syllabi, and texts; such enormous impact is reason enough for assessing them. I also think that coming to terms with our own theories will help us to assimilate work in other fields more efficiently.

To look at these theories together is to appreciate what might seem at first implausible: that as diverse as they are these are not simply four unrelated theories but theories capable of being interpreted in retrospect as evincing an underlying, developmental logic—specifically a Hegelian logic. How I see the interrelationships among these theories will also shed light on why I have analyzed them in a sequence not strictly chronological.

In the nineteenth century, as many historians have affirmed, the classical heritage of systematic knowledge about discourse in general and rhetoric in particular fragmented and lost vitality after two millennia of cultural dominance. There are many reasons for this decline, but so far as this study is concerned the causes matter less than the result, which might be fairly described as a regression to a "folklore" or "prephilosophical" condition. The discipline became a patchwork composed largely of ill-sorted pieces from classical rhetoric, from Ramism, and from certain eighteenth-century theorists, such as Alexander Bain. This state of conceptual chaos confronted the revival of rhetoric that began in English departments around 1960.

Most of us who have studied rhetoric since that time have been taught to see the discipline as gaining ground insofar as it moves away from the product orientation of the "current-traditional paradigm" and toward the various process approaches that have increasingly dominated recent theory. On the whole, this self-understanding is serviceable enough, but I would like to complicate the picture somewhat by suggesting that the initial move was not so much toward process as it was toward overcoming the conceptual confusion of the American school-rhetoric tradition. In other words, the first step was to regain some degree of philosophical coherence for a field that had little of it.

As Hegel said, the initial impulse of philosophy, the way it moves beyond folklore, is conceptual analysis and clarification. *Verstand* 'the understanding' performs this valuable service in being concerned primarily with eliminating the overlap and interrelation among concepts used casually and without precision. Kinneavy's theory is obviously dedicated to this task. That is why it is dominated by surveys of past concepts, comparisons of conceptual schemes, typologies of discourse, and other efforts to overcome such loose usages as the catch-all category, exposition. Britton's work (e.g., the discourse functions and audience types) also pursues this end, if less saliently and single-mindedly than Kinneavy's does.

No field can progress very far without the understanding's work. At the same time, the effort to fix concepts produces its own problems. Neatly delimited categories, reified and cut off from one another, cannot handle developmental or temporal dimensions. To enable his conceptual advance, Kinneavy had to turn away from the process implications of composition. And so for Kinneavy's thesis there is Moffett's antithesis. The thrust of *Teaching the Universe of Discourse* is to counter the very kind of thinking that results in categories and departments. For instance, while Moffett clearly recognizes distinctions between speech and writing, he focuses on their overlap and interrelation and on the development from collaborative conversation to going it alone, delivering a speech or composing a paper. He makes fixed categories fluid because he has to, because his developmental approach to discourse requires seeing how *a* actually becomes *b*, not just how *a* may be distinguished from *b*.

Kinneavy's way of thinking about discourse, centered in the understanding and concentrated on the analysis of finished discourses, is antithetical to Moffett's way, but the two are not mutually exclusive, and this fact is crucial to overcoming the simplistic product-process dichotomy. Excepting his interest in the history of discourse, Kinneavy is product-oriented. But his thinking is also complementary to Moffett's process orientation. That is, if we cannot distinguish *a* from *b* we cannot talk about their interrelation or development from the one state to the other. Britton appreciated this logic when he pointed out that we require both a static model of adult discourse types and a developmental model of progression toward mature competence. As we shall see in due course, Britton is in some significant ways the synthesis of Kinneavy's thesis and Moffett's antithesis, especially in combining Kinneavy's typological preoccupations with Moffett's developmental concerns.

D'Angelo's place in the developmental logic of our four theories is rather complex. On the one hand, in his respect for classical rhetoric, in his structuralism, and in his frequent use of discourse analysis, D'Angelo is close to Kinneavy. On the other hand, he shares with Moffett and Britton a concern with process, but the thought process rather than process in the sense of a learning sequence or process in the sense of the acts of composing. One must admit that *A Conceptual Theory of Rhetoric* breaks out of the triad and spoils the symmetry, but that deviation seems healthy to me. I am suggesting a Hegelian logic, not as a schema within which to force everything to fit, but rather as a way to move past the seeming randomness of our theoretical work. It helps, but it is not some magical device that reconciles everything. D'Angelo's theory forces us to think outside triads; it also will help us ask how discourse theory relates to rhetorical theory, an important but seldom-asked question.

My sequence, in sum, is to pose a thesis in Kinneavy; an antithesis in Moffett; a partial, inadequate synthesis in Britton; and, finally, while not discarding the notion of progressive unfolding altogether, taking up D'Angelo as a significant if problematical "other," someone that belongs in our argument even if he wants to change the subject a bit. All this is part 1. Part 2 is my own synthesis; I believe that it moves us a step or two beyond where we would be without it, beyond, at least, our four theories. But I offer it in all modesty; without Kinneavy, Britton, Moffett, and D'Angelo I could never have thought it, and it does not make much sense without them. Moreover, it is far from being a final, definitive *aufgehoben*. Rather I would call it a talking point, an invitation for further discussion.

ANALYSIS OF THE THEORIES

PREVIEW OF PART 1

Part 1 involves fairly intricate arguments about the central concepts of each theory. It may be helpful, therefore, to preview these concepts and the main conclusions reached in my analysis of them.

Kinneavy

Much of the Kinneavy chapter grapples with the concept of aim or purpose. Basically, I argue that aim is a judgment often requiring argumentative justification, not an objective property of a text or a bundle of features that one can simply point to. It follows, then, that aim is not a generic concept, reliable for distinguishing discourse classes. Rather, it is a concept with heuristic value, useful primarily as a way of sorting out discourse genres in a particular time and place.

In short, although I think we need some concept of aim or function, Kinneavy's treatment of the concept is unconvincing. I also hold, with one of Kinneavy's critics, that aim cannot be construed, in Kinneavy's words, as "largely determining everything in a text." I argue instead that Britton's multidimensionality hypothesis, which treats aim as one of many significant variables, merits our tentative acceptance.

I then discuss Kinneavy's descriptions of the individual aims. I defend his oral-based, Aristotelian approach to persuasion, conceding that some instances of written persuasion may well require supplementing his view with, for example, Chaim Perelman's work on philosophical argumentation. I also defend Kinneavy's distinctions between expression and exploration in the face of efforts to collapse these two ends of discourse into one.

Finally, I question Kinneavy's uncritical use of Aristotle's distinction between demonstration and argument, truth and opinion, as a way of distinguishing science from rhetoric. In essence, we will see that science and rhetoric differ not as certainty differs from probability, or truth from the appearance of truth, but rather in social, pragmatic terms, as, for instance, in what counts as evidential adequacy.

The last part of chapter 1 focuses on Kinneavy's concept of mode. While endorsing his effort to ground modality in explicit conceptual terms, I dispute his effort to distinguish language from the extramental world, and I find his four modes and their subdivisions unsatisfying. I urge, therefore, a rethinking of modality in the light of the problems uncovered.

In the Kinneavy chapter I also address the structuralism of all four theories. The critical assault on structuralism cannot be ignored, of course, but the typological requirements of discourse theory will scarcely permit us to abandon structuralism altogether. And so what I advocate is a critical structuralism, one that recognizes its limitations and systematically compensates for them.

Moffett

In significant respects Moffett's theory is counterstructural and thus overcomes some of the limitations of typological thought. In my view, the chief and enduring contribution of *Teaching the Universe of Discourse* is not its idea of a learning sequence, a very old, indeed, ancient idea that Moffett updates by incorporating Jean Piaget's theories, but its brilliant demonstration of how to think about discourse in developmental, rather than merely categorical, terms. Whereas Kinneavy's system would classify, say, a history, a scientific tract, and a philosophical treatise as merely so many instances of reference discourse, Moffett's approach would allow us to see their interrelations, especially with respect to abstractive altitude, or distance from immediate experience. Whereas Kinneavy tends to take the speech-writing distinction as simply two kinds of media, Moffett works with the dynamic relations between, especially, conversation and composition: how the former becomes the latter, how the latter can grow out of and return to the former. The first part of the Moffett chapter explores several of the many ways he dissolves or displaces categorical thought; it also celebrates his integrated theory, integrated in the sense that drama is both the source of all forms of discourse and the informing metaphor for a classroom filled with discourse activity, rather than mere talk about discourse.

On the other side, I criticize Moffett's neglect of aim or purpose, which among other problems leads him to undervalue persuasive discourse and to contradict himself in the handling of literature. Closely related to having no aim or function model is Moffett's overconstricted view of the I-it relation as adequately approachable in terms of information processing. While information processing is certainly useful, it is severely limited in handling most kinds of discourse.

In comparing Moffett's handling of literature with Kinneavy's, I consider the still-debatable status of literature, that is, whether it belongs properly to aesthetics or to discourse. The gist of my position is that efforts to make a special case of literature in order to exempt it from discursive evaluation introduce criteria that would also prohibit us from taking much nonliterary discourse as discourse. Arguing, then, for literature as a kind of discourse for which aesthetic assessment is especially but not exclusively appropriate, I attempt to show that Moffett is the only one of our theorists to escape from the objectivist-formalist view of literature. Moffett says that literature is discourse, and he treats literature as discourse, not only as an object to contemplate in itself but as an act that challenges our horizon of understanding.

Britton

With Britton we reach both a temporary resting point and a host of difficult choices. On the one hand, Britton combines Kinneavy's typological concern, missing from Moffett's work, with Moffett's developmental concern, wholly neglected by Kinneavy. The result is a model of mature discourse functions linked with at least the beginnings of a developmental model of the functions, starting with immature expression, moving to expressive discourse, and continuing to the transactional (informative, persuasive) and poetic uses of language. On the other hand, as we shall see in some detail, Britton's discourse functions clash in some subtle and some not so subtle ways with Kinneavy's aims, forcing careful discriminations and ultimately some hard decisions.

In a close comparison of the aim-function schemes, I argue that the implications of aim accord better than function with the needs of a discourse typology. Accordingly, I favor the use of aim, reinterpreted in a nonobjective fashion. Against Kinneavy, however, I show that Britton's multidimensionality hypothesis is preferable to Kinneavy's overemphasis on aim as the chief and controlling discourse variable. Moreover, I also advance Britton's notion of continua between the aims over Kinneavy's foreground-background approach, mainly because the continua approach encourages more subtle discriminations of mixed purposes in actual discourses.

Against Britton I hold that his dichotomizing of the poetic and transactional functions overidealizes. I also offer reasons to reject the centrality of expressive discourse for our model of the mature aims, favoring Kinneavy's more neutral view, which sees expression as just one of four aims, each one of value in its own right. I also reaffirm Kinneavy's carefully reasoned distinctions between exploratory and expressive discourse, which Britton's treatment tends to muddle, and I point to Kinneavy's focus on public, group expression (e.g., the manifesto or declaration) as a kind of discourse Britton does not recognize.

In addition, Britton recognizes a kind of discourse that Kinneavy overlooked, the regulative (e.g., a set of instructions or orders). Since this kind of discourse is audience-centered but not persuasive, I argue that Britton's category "conative" with its two subdivisions, "regulative" and "persuasive," is preferable to Kinneavy's persuasive category alone. I also think that Britton's view of the range of exploratory discourse may have advantages over Kinneavy's tendency to see exploration as either dialogue or scientific theorizing.

Besides pulling together the strengths of Kinneavy and Moffett, Britton's theory has other virtues. To the extent that we have a developmental view of the aims at all, Britton has provided it. He also proffers the best theory of audience among our four theorists and is the only one to address the key variable of writer's attitude toward the writing task.

As in the first two chapters, I pose one issue of general significance that arises implicitly from the theory under consideration but is not addressed by any of our theorists. In Britton's theory the issue is, How fine-grained should our discourse typologies be? How far ought we to take the effort to subcategorize within the aims? This question almost poses itself when we consider Britton's treatment of informative discourse, which Kinneavy did not subdivide at all but which Britton subdivides into seven categories. In brief, my answer is that development of a theory in this dimension depends on application rather than on theory itself. As Britton found it necessary to distinguish many kinds of informative discourse in order to handle the high percentage of student scripts allotted to this aim in his study, so there are many good reasons in practice to subcategorize within any of the aims. But the matter of how fine-grained our categories should be cannot be answered on theoretical grounds alone.

D'Angelo

D'Angelo's study resembles Kinneavy's in being strongly structuralist and informed by the ancient rhetorical tradition, but it shares as well the Moffett-

Britton concern with cognition. D'Angelo's focus, however, is not on cognitive development and its relation to discoursing ability; rather, D'Angelo seeks a science of rhetoric grounded in a science of mind. In the context of our other three theories, *A Conceptual Theory of Rhetoric* suggests a key question: What notion of rhetoric best complements our theories of discourse?

On the negative side, while recognizing the value of scientific studies of discourse and discourse processes, I criticize D'Angelo for trying to turn the art of rhetoric into a science and for holding that one of the main tasks of the teacher is to convey theory. I agree with Kinneavy's view of rhetoric, which is really Aristotle's, and with Moffett's view that theory, although critical to the formation of curricula and syllabi, is secondary in the classroom to actual discoursing. Also questionable is D'Angelo's understanding of the relation between language and perception and between language and thought. I argue that human perception is far more language-saturated than D'Angelo recognizes and that language and thought cannot be usefully distinguished. I affirm Lev Vygotsky's view that language and thought merge at a very early stage in human development, that our primary concern is not their relation but rather how "inner speech" becomes composing—becomes public discourse.

On the positive side, D'Angelo has the only *process* view of aim among our four theorists. Whereas Kinneavy sees aim as "final cause," D'Angelo sees it as part of the sense of the whole that writers either have as they begin to write or discover en route. Reinterpreting D'Angelo's topoi as dialectical rather than rhetorical, I praise him for rescuing the "places" from their textbook reduction to methods of paragraph development, for recognizing that invention is much more than logic (something that Kinneavy does not sufficiently emphasize), and for ordering his topics in a way that avoids a mere checklist (as in Aristotle). However, I dispute D'Angelo's attempt to show that there is a kind of cognitive "deep structure" that permits him to equate rhetoric's three "offices," invention, arrangement, and style. I believe that there is overlap and interrelation, but not identity.

Addressing the main question of this chapter—how to relate discourse theory to rhetoric—I urge thinking of rhetoric primarily in the plural, as rhetorics needed for the aims and subaims our discourse theories discriminate. This means, of course, a view of rhetoric closer to Kinneavy's than D'Angelo's, and consonant with Britton's view that "writing cannot be regarded globally" (10).

Part 1 is devoted to theoretical assessment: close comparison of similar concepts, reconceptualization where necessary, and relation of concepts not previously thought of as being related. The method is argument, the good reasons for preferring one formulation to another. Its spirit is permanent revisionism, striving ever for the better in pursuit of that which is always out of reach, the best. Its guiding assumption is that we must overcome the product-process dichotomy by developing all leading concepts in both dimensions.

CHAPTER ONE

KINNEAVY'S THEORY

Overview

Two basic concepts dominate Kinneavy's theory: the aims (ends, purposes) of discourse and the modes (means) of discourse.

Kinneavy deduces his aims from the minimal elements of every discourse act:

encoder   (a writer or speaker)
decoder   (a readership or audience)
signal   (written or spoken words in meaningful sequences)
reality   (that which the signal refers to, the world external to mind)

Thus, encoder-centered discourse is expressive; decoder-centered, persuasive; signal-centered, literary; and reality-centered, referential. Expression takes in, for example, diaries, journals, much informal conversation; persuasion embraces editorials, public speeches, advertising; literature includes drama, poetry, fiction, jokes; and referential discourse covers most business and technical communication, scientific writing, news stories, and so on.

There are further subdivisions within referential discourse (explanatory, informative, and scientific) and within expression (individual and group), but Kinneavy does not systematically discriminate subtypes within the other two aims. In essence, *A Theory of Discourse* attempts to describe each aim, its history, its characteristic logic, organization, and style.

Kinneavy sharply distinguishes aim from mode. The modes are *not* related to the communication triangle (18–20); they derive, rather, from three basic philosophical distinctions: between being and becoming, essence and existence, and potency and act (Kinneavy et al., *Modes* 10–14).

The four modes—narration, description, classification, evaluation—divide first into modes of being and modes of becoming. The modes of being are description and classification. Description deals with being because it would isolate the distinctive features of something; classification deals with being because it would establish the class membership of something, as in genus/species definition. Narration obviously is a mode of becoming; so also is evaluation, for it attempts to judge something in relation to some notion of potential.

The two modes of being differ from each other according to the existence-essence pair. When I describe something, I am dealing with it existentially, as it appears to me here and now, as a bracketed entity (i.e., in itself). For example, I may describe a particular man I met. But I may also try to classify this person by calling him an American, a medical doctor, a neo-Kantian. In each case, I am dealing with an essence, not a simple, present, observable item like eye color, but a high-level abstraction.

The two modes of becoming divide according to potency/act. When I tell a story, I am making actual a certain potential in the characters and situations. When I evaluate, I take the completed act, for example, a book or a movie, and judge it according to how well it realizes itself, lives up to its potential, as we say. Thus, both narration and evaluation are matters of potency/act, but from different perspectives, the former making actual a potential, the latter praising or blaming an act according to its potential.

Thus carefully discriminated from each other and derived from distinctions having nothing to do with the minimal elements of the discourse act, Kinneavy hopes to avoid two common problems: a mere ad hoc list of modes and the confusion of the aims of discourse with the purposes of discourse. Because of their grounding in philosophical concepts, Kinneavy's modes are not ad hoc. Because he stresses the subordination of modes to aims, there should be no confusion of purpose with means of realizing purpose. For instance, narration exists not in itself but as a story or process recounted for some reason—to entertain, to persuade, to inform.

Finally, Kinneavy emphasizes the notion of predominance with respect to both the aims and the modes. Any particular discourse will most likely mix two or more aims and modes. "Pure" illustrative instances are perhaps even impossible to find in any extended discourse. Therefore, to use Kinneavy's typology, one must always make a judgment about foreground and background, realizing that to some extent all the aims and all the modes are usually present.

Analysis

The Nature of Aim

What exactly is the status of aim in Kinneavy's theory? On the one hand, Kinneavy wants to objectify aim, saying that it is "embodied in the text itself." On the other hand, if aim implies an objective target, something aimed at (a discourse of a certain kind), it also implies subjectivity, that someone is taking aim; hence, Kinneavy says, "the intent of the author . . . partially determines the aim of the discourse." In the final analysis, however, he seems to settle on an objective status for aim, "given the qualifications of situation and culture" obviously not "in the text itself" (*Theory* 49).

As the references to W. K. Wimsatt establish, Kinneavy was driven to this objectivist position by the logic of New Criticism, which would proscribe both intent and affect as reliable guides to assessing literature. Kinneavy was educated in the New Critical tradition and was essentially a New Critic when he wrote *Theory*. Now that the New Criticism has lost its theoretical hold on our discipline, the way is open to reassess aim apart from the strictures of the so-called intentional and affective fallacies.

Although the two questions are closely related, we ought not to confuse aim itself with the problem of arriving at knowledge of aim. Aim is a judgment, an interpretation of motive. As a reader I infer the dominant aim of a text, in Kinneavy's words, from "a totality of effect generated by the things talked about, the organization given the materials, the accompanying style, and so on" (*Theory* 49). If I happen to know something about a discourse's context, such knowledge may also influence my judgment. As a writer I interpret my own motives as I attempt to adapt what I have to say for a particular audience and situation. But whether I am reading or writing, aim is interpretation. It is not in the text. It is not even precisely in me, either, though I must draw the inferences and make the judgment. Aim is, rather, a matter of recognizing conventions, the collective frame of normative expectations. It is only in such a framework that a set of stylistic features can add up to anything that will allow us to draw inferences about aim. Only such a framework can guide us as writers in estimating what this audience or that situation calls for where aim is concerned.

If aim is an interpretation rather than something "in" a text, it may seem that reliable knowledge about aim becomes an impossibility. If aim is not an objective concept, it is not a scientific concept. Perhaps such a notion was behind Kinneavy's attempt to objectivize aim, since he worked from a basically scientific model (i.e., the semiotic "communication triangle").

But, of course, all knowledge involves interpretation; nothing comes to us unmediated. If reliable knowledge about aim is sometimes hard to come by, the difficulty does not lie in aim's being an interpretation per se. The difficulty lies instead in the nature of motive itself: often we are not sure of our own motives, as they are usually mixed, ambiguous, ambivalent, and of variable intensity; nor are we always sure that we are correctly reading the signs of conventional motives, since sometimes the conventions themselves are changing rapidly, and even firmly established and relatively enduring conventions may be deliberately manipulated to achieve, for example, an ironic effect.

As in any other case in which a judgment is challenged, we must be prepared to defend our interpretations of aim. The aim of discourse cannot be established just by pointing out textual features. Aim is not simply an empirical issue, something that can be settled by calculation or by observation alone. Aim must be argued for; the worth of our judgment of aim in any particular case is the sum of the good reasons we can adduce in support of it.

The Function of Aim

Kinneavy's main criticism of most recent approaches to teaching discourse is their neglect of the liberal arts tradition, which "represented an attempt to train people to various and important uses of language" (*Theory* 28). Instead of teaching persuasive discourse, for example, these approaches tend to orient instruction toward the modes of discourse or the "arts" of discourse (i.e., the language arts: reading, speaking, listening, writing). Hence the comparison-contrast essay, which treats the modes of comparison and contrast as if they were ends in themselves rather than means that one might use to inform, persuade; hence the teaching of reading as if no distinctions were to be made between reading for information and reading, say, a poem. In short, Kinneavy holds that aim (end, purpose) is usually neglected.

Consequently, Kinneavy claims that

> [p]urpose in discourse is all important. The aim of a discourse determines everything else in the process of discourse. "What" is talked about, the oral or written medium which is chosen, the words and grammatical patterns used—all of these are largely determined by the purpose of the discourse. (*Theory* 48)

In a recent article, Richard Fulkerson rightly says that this hypothesis about the centrality of aim amounts to Kinneavy's *theory* of discourse as distinct from his particular typology of aims (43). Though, of course, Kinneavy's assumption that aim is the main controlling variable of discourse leads directly to his typology, one might agree that aim is all important and not adhere to Kinneavy's division of aims; conversely, one might accept Kinneavy's typology while holding that other variables, such as audience, also condition choices in the process of writing. The assertion about aim, then, is more or less distinct from the aims themselves.

It is difficult to escape the conclusion that Kinneavy's emphasis on aim amounts to a dialectical overcompensation. If Kinneavy had said only that purpose is all important, perhaps no objections would arise, since what we try to do in a discourse is certainly one major factor we hold in mind as we write. But to say that aim determines everything else—even if qualified by "largely"—is to overstate the case. As Fulkerson points out (49), Kinneavy himself admits that subject matter, not aim, often structures scientific writing. One can add that, while to some extent audiences are implied by aim, there is still a range of variation within, say, audiences for informative discourse. *The World Book Encyclopedia* differs from *Britannica* in part because the former is directed to a younger audience.

Audience is not the only variable related to aim and yet sufficiently independent of it to elude determination by it. A roundtable discussion, for instance, will require one type of argument; a published article, quite another. The linguistic ability and general experience I possess will also constrain what I can say or write more or less independently of my aim. And so on. If there is no variable more important than aim, there are many that are no less important. The theoretical hegemony of aim, then, cannot be accepted.

It is obvious that I favor the view of aim that Britton calls function. Basically, he takes it as one of many interdependent factors that condition choices made by writers. In my view, instead of embracing Kinneavy's hierarchical view that has aim determining everything else, we must opt for Britton's multidimensionality hypothesis, discussed in chapter 3.

In fairness to Kinneavy, we should grant that the context in which he was writing probably called for overstressing aim. At the same time, theory will be better served if we recognize that discourse is too complex for any treatment based on a single principle.

The Scope of Aim

We have said that aim is a judgment. But what kind of concept is it? Kinneavy treats aim as if it designated a genus, a class of existents. I think we will see, however, that the aim concept is really heuristic, not generic;

in itself, aim leads to useful questions about discourse produced in some time or place, but until it is applied to such discourse, it has no classificatory value.

Consider, for example, Kinneavy's handling of scientific discourse. Wishing to avoid ethnocentricity, Kinneavy opens the aim to discourse distant from us in time—"some myths, legends, folklore, religious cosmologies, and past metaphysics can be valid corpora of scientific discourse"—and also distant from us in place or cultural heritage—"Russian lexicography, French existentialism, Subanum medicine, Esquimau physics, German literary theory, and Buddhist theology are also bona fide specimens of scientific discourse" (*Theory* 78).

Such a view is salutary, of course. If, however, one is serious about accepting any "attempt to represent the universe and to demonstrate, somehow or another, the validity" (78) of the representation as scientific discourse, one must give up the very idea of describing the distinctive features or even the norms of such a genus. Breadth has been bought at the price of vacuity.

The potential bind that Kinneavy faces turns up by implication on the very page where he takes so expansive a view of science. He refers to the logic of demonstration. As no one need tell him, such a logic (at least as a formalized system) is not significantly older than Aristotle's apodictic proof. The preliterate mind that produced most of our myths and religious cosmologies had no logic of demonstration—had, indeed, no formal logic whatsoever. As Walter Ong has shown at length, both science and formal logic depend on writing (*Orality* 105, 107). Therefore, we must either exclude part of what Kinneavy is willing to take as science or hold that demonstration is not a generic norm for scientific discourse.

Kinneavy "resolves" the dilemma here exposed practically, silently, without addressing the theoretical issues involved. As an English-speaking person steeped in Western culture and speaking to an audience similarly situated, he need have no thought of Buddhist theology or Esquimau physics when he describes scientific discourse. Rather, he is thinking of what Thomas Kuhn calls normal science, discourses that seek to confirm or disprove prevailing paradigms (Kuhn 10); he is thinking of mainline, modern instances of scientific discourse. Thus localized, the heuristic aim concept can become genuinely generic. Ludwig Wittgenstein's useful metaphor of family resemblance can take hold (31e–32e).

At root, the difficulties of scope, where Kinneavy's aims are concerned, are the difficulties of structuralism generally. The semiotic communication triangle, from which the aims are derived, is classically structuralist in that it is composed of timeless, placeless, nearly contentless elements. As virtually pure abstraction, the triangle is a figure in space, eternal, fixed, gestaltlike—in short, it is everything discourse is not, since discourse is rooted in speech, in sound, and therefore in time, in history, and in culture. Each language community produces its own distinctive types of discourse; each type has its own, never-to-be-repeated evolution. That is why the aims take in so much that nothing distinguishable remains. That is why they must be applied to discourse somehow localized in time and space before generic properties can emerge. Their nature and value, therefore, are heuristic, leading to questions like, What forms does scientific discourse take in the modern Western world?

All four of our theories were produced in the heyday of structuralism; all four are to varying degrees structuralist. The liabilities and assets of this approach, then, are scarcely restricted to Kinneavy. Given the recent theoretical assault on structuralism, perhaps a few comments are in order on how I view structuralism for the purposes of this study.

Structuralism is an essentialist strategy of thought. It seeks some underlying coherence to account for the bewildering variety of phenomena and the transmutations of form in time. It is opposed, therefore, by those who attack the very concept of essence, who seek the truth in concrete manifestation, who assert, in effect, that there is nothing but the void beneath what shows itself to us. Hence, structuralism is usually ignored or rejected by traditional historical scholars, phenomenologists, and existentialists and usually embraced, at least implicitly, by nearly all scientific thought. In its search for a bedrock foundation to explain and control, structuralism's line extends back to Descartes and ultimately to Plato. The antistructuralists belong to the so-called process and life philosophies, to figures such as Nietzsche, Heidegger, Bergson, and Whitehead.

Led by Kenneth Burke's reflections on language, I hold that both structure and process are implicit in language and therefore in thought. Every time we name something, we are willy-nilly essentialists; and yet, our assertions always are uttered or written in time and responded to in time and are therefore of a piece with historical process. Hence, my tactics throughout this study are dialectical: I assume that the structuralist "moment" requires the antistructuralist one and that what we must do is seize on the best that each has to offer in an effort to move beyond them to an ever more adequate synthesis. For this reason, though I have offered several revisions of Kinneavy's aim concept, these revisions certainly do not imply rejection of either the aims or the structuralism behind them.

The Individual Aims

One might think that the problem of scope relative to the aim concept would adversely affect Kinneavy's descriptions of the individual aims. There may be some minor strain here and there resulting from the clash of abstract concept and localized application, but by and large Kinneavy avoids dissonance by dealing with discourse relatively close to us in place and time. The problems with Kinneavy's descriptions of the aims derive from a different source altogether—namely, his overdependence on ancient sources, especially Aristotle, for description of the aims.

Persuasion. Kinneavy's reliance on Aristotle is most obvious in the chapter on persuasion, which amounts to a rewriting of the *Rhetoric.* Here we find all the familiar Aristotelian terminology coupled with awareness of new genres of persuasion unknown to the ancients, such as advertising. The implication is, therefore, that Aristotle's treatment is basically all we need to handle any instance of persuasive discourse.

As everyone knows, Aristotle was thinking of public speaking—oral persuasion—directed at a general audience of Athenian citizens. Kinneavy's choice of Roosevelt's first inaugural address as an exemplar fits the Aristotelian terminology well. But how about written persuasion directed at a select readership?

How one might answer this question is by no means obvious. It is reasonable to assume, however, that written persuasion can risk more intricate reasoning than oral persuasion can, simply because the former can be reread and studied. It seems likely that a sophisticated readership would respond less to emotional appeal and more to logical cogency. One can see the broad differences here by comparing Martin Luther King's "Letter from Birmingham Jail" with his "I Have a Dream" speech.

But do the differences between oral and written persuasion amount to differences of degree or of kind? Fulkerson rejects Kinneavy's oral model for persuasion and attacks his Aristotelian view of persuasive logic as a "watered down" version of formal or scientific reasoning (50). For Fulkerson, then, the differences are ones of kind, which would justify a break with the categories of classical rhetoric. But Kinneavy would hold that the differences are only differences of degree, that written persuasion uses the same tactics as oral persuasion does but in different proportions and with different emphases.

Because of the impact of Ong's books, linguistic studies of dialects and grapholects, and such work by people in our field as *Exploring Speaking and Writing Relationships* (Kroll and Vann), we have become acutely aware of the distinction between oral and written discourse. Certainly, the distinction is significant, since the oral and the written differ from each other not only superficially, in terms of quantifiable features, but also at a deeper, more pervasive level; the written word has a noetic and social impact amounting to the transformation of culture itself. As teachers of writing, we are acutely concerned about the differences between orality and literacy, particularly since many of our students come to us only marginally literate. This makes understandable, then, the probable source and the appeal of Fulkerson's rejection of Kinneavy's oral model of persuasion.

In this instance, however, the case for Kinneavy's approach seems to me the stronger. A careful reading of Ong's work will show that his insistence on the differences between orality and literacy is matched by an equally strong claim for the primacy of the oral, the ultimate source of all discourse (*Orality* 7). Such primacy is especially obvious in persuasion, which is historically oral. According to Ong, anything that we would recognize as scientific discourse belongs to the world of literacy; however, persuasion long predates a written art of rhetoric and may even be virtually coeval with language itself. Persuasion's special affinity for the spoken word is also evident in preliterate children, who often evince amazing persuasive ability. It may well be, then, that Kinneavy's orality-based approach to persuasion is appropriate to the basic nature of the aim.

Independent support for Kinneavy's reliance on Aristotle also comes from *The New Rhetoric* (Perelman and Olbrechts-Tyteca). Chaim Perelman was explicitly concerned with written persuasion; after ten years of study, he concluded that what he had basically done was rediscover Aristotle, especially Aristotle's dialectic, rhetoric's antistrophe, or counterpart (5). Granted, Perelman also rejected the Aristotelian view of rhetorical reasoning as a "loose" or simplified version of formal reasoning; he contended that the two are incommensurable and complementary, differing mainly in that rhetorical reasoning establishes and justifies the realm of value. Therefore, Fulkerson's resistance to Kinneavy's treatment of logos in written persuasion is seconded by Perelman's followers. Like Kinneavy, however, Perelman will not allow that rhetoric can even approach apodictic proof. The closest rhetoric can come to formal logic is in certain "quasi-logical arguments," which have the form but not the compelling quality of formal reasoning (193). So, for example, the long section about law in King's "Letter" is carefully, even rigorously, argued, but it hinges on a distinction between traditional law and natural or God-ordained law which is fundamentally disputable, which eludes formal demonstration altogether.

In sum, then, Kinneavy's approach to persuasion in oral, Aristotelian terms is not fundamentally misdirected. Indeed, in some respects, it is superior to Perelman's treatment, for even written persuasion for relatively sophisticated audiences uses pathetic appeal, an aspect of rhetoric Perelman chooses to underplay in his account, but which Kinneavy, following Aristotle, emphasizes. Kinneavy also, because of his reliance on Aristotle, does a much better job with stylistic appeal.

Because persuasion has especially deep roots in orality, Kinneavy's approach cannot be fundamentally misdirected. But when we consider written and printed instances, especially when they are directed at sophisticated groups or at Perelman's universal audience, Kinneavy's treatment of logos especially is just not adequate and must be supplemented, for example, by Perelman's revisions and extensions of classical rhetoric. We obviously cannot approach philosophical persuasion with exactly the same attitudes and expectations that we approach, for example, television advertising.

Scientific Discourse. Kinneavy's adherence to Aristotelian distinctions is also obvious in his treatment of scientific discourse. Basically, Kinneavy holds with Aristotle that there is such a thing as demonstration or apodictic proof that attains certainty by a combination of strict, formal reasoning and empirical method. According to Kinneavy, the contrast between demonstration and argument, between reasoning that can attain certainty and reasoning that begins and ends in probability, is one of the main differences between scientific and persuasive discourse.

The distinction itself would appear fundamentally suspect after the work of Thomas Kuhn. If science progresses by revolution, by more or less radical changes in the paradigms held by a particular science, then how can one say that science attains certainty? Even if Kuhn is wrong in some respects in his account of scientific revolutions, it can scarcely be denied that the demonstrations that once confirmed Newtonian physics are now seen to require reinterpretation in the light of Einstein's hypotheses. Science, then, is permanently open-ended, a condition seemingly incompatible with the implications of certainty.

Thought along these lines probably accounts for most of the resistance to Kinneavy's treatment of scientific discourse. Because for Kinneavy scientific discourse includes neither the articulation of hypotheses (which belongs to exploratory discourse) nor the dissemination of scientific knowledge and its implications to the general public (which belongs to informative discourse or sometimes persuasive discourse), the function of the aim in effect is limited to demonstration, limited, in fact, to the great bulk of work one can find in the professional journals. Therefore, the status of demonstration is indeed pivotal.

Unfortunately, Kinneavy is not clear about exactly how or to what extent science attains certainty. He seems content with the general distinction between *episteme* 'knowledge' and *pistis* 'opinion, belief,' seeing the former as the aim of science, the latter as the aim of rhetoric or persuasion. While perhaps in a rough and ready way this Aristotelian distinction is still useful, it requires much qualification and explanation to be sufficient. For instance, Aristotle himself recognized that science must have first principles or assumptions that science itself cannot demonstrate. Science must assume that the universe is ordered and more or less uniform. Obviously, no amount of evidence can establish such a belief; here, at the outset, *pistis* in one of its meanings (i.e., faith) enters the picture, as Michael Polanyi insists (266–67). Science also assumes that all phenomena ultimately have their grounding in physics, in materialist categories of explanation. The effort to reduce mind to brain, for example, is comprehensible only within such an assumption. Again, one can scarcely hope to demonstrate in any rigorous, compelling way the truth of a materialist metaphysic. At the level of assumption, then, science is no more certain than persuasion, and King's distinction between God's law and our law is exactly as disputable as the attempt to deny any distinction between brain and mind.

Assumptions, of course, are by their very nature uncertain; otherwise, we would not have to assume them. Also permanently beyond demonstration are the paradigms Kuhn discusses, the level of scientific theory. If theory could be completely demonstrated, it would no longer be theory: therefore, science does not attain certainty at the level of comprehensive explanation either.

Strictly, then, one must hold that scientific deduction produces certainty only within a framework of uncertain assumptions and hypotheses. If, that is, x and y are assumed, and if hypothesis z is held as provisionally true, then deduction a follows. The problem, of course, is that even scientists are prone to forget that assumptions are assumptions and that their theories are only theories, since they operate habitually within what Whitehead called the "current abstractions" (Moffett 28). Kinneavy contributes to this forgetfulness and to the consequent turning of science into a kind of secular faith by not examining carefully enough the kind of certainty science does achieve.

What kind of certainty does science achieve? For instance, it is difficult to see how or why anyone would doubt that the basic atomic structure of water is H_2O. One may doubt that the statement is significant within certain frames of reference, but not that it is true. Every scientific field has many such indubitable assertions, which we might as well call, in accord with common usage, *fact*. About the only common problem at this level is that care must be taken in the statement of so-called scientific facts. One may say, There is a high correlation between cigarette smoking and the incidence of lung cancer, for more than enough evidence confirms such a statement, but one may not say, Smoking causes cancer, the typical public construction of this "scientific fact." Another level of certainty may be found in the strict meaning of scientific law, such as the laws of thermodynamics. Again, it is hard to see how or why anyone would deny laws confirmed over and over again by common observation and controlled experiment.

The existence of fact and law in science does not alter, of course, the doubtful nature of the assumptions and theories of science. As the mention of evidence in the last paragraph suggests, science differs from persuasion not on the basis of certainty as opposed to probability but on the kind of proof admissible as generally accepted norms of the aim. In persuasion, an example or two, whether historical or fictive, may suffice; in science, examples may be used to suggest the potential explanatory power of a hypothesis in exploratory discourse, but they would not be advanced or accepted as an effort at demonstration in scientific discourse. Induction in scientific demonstration must conform to certain well-recognized conventions, as Kinneavy points out (*Theory* 109–18).

If Kinneavy is unclear about what constitutes certainty in science, he is clear enough about what qualifies as evidence in scientific demonstration. And the latter is mainly what we must be aware of to understand the typical features of scientific discourse. Science relies, on the one hand, on various kinds of formal, especially mathematical, reasoning, which constitutes its deductive procedures; it relies, on the other hand, on methods such as controlled laboratory experiment for empirical confirmation of hypothetical constructs, which constitutes its inductive procedures. Neither produces certainty: deduction is capable only of making explicit what is implicit in one's premises; induction is capable, at best, of a warrantable assumption of high probability. Together, however, they do produce most of the distinguishing features of scientific discourse conceived as efforts at scientific demonstration.

In sum, then, one can say that scientific discourse comprises discourses that attempt to test hypotheses generated within a paradigm, usually by some method that can in one sense or another be called empirical. In other words, the published work of "normal science" is scientific discourse. Thus interpreted, we have a useful category that scientists worldwide will recognize as typical of their professional discourse, as peers to peers.

It must be admitted that in so construing scientific discourse I am not in complete accord with Kinneavy. Apparently, he is willing to allow a broader range of discourse as scientific, since he analyzes an excerpt from Camus's novel *The Rebel* as an illustration of deductive argument (119–26). In my view, the Camus excerpt is an instance of written persuasion for a relatively sophisticated audience; it is not scientific discourse and would not be accepted as such by most scientists. Here again we see the problem of scope where Kinneavy's aims are concerned. If we treat the Camus excerpt as science, we shall have to open the aim to virtually all philosophical argument, including Hegel's science of logic, the metaphysical nature of which no contemporary scientist could accept as science. Such a move impoverishes the category by breadth; confuses scientific discourse with philosophy, which neither philosopher nor scientist can welcome; and makes description of the aim impossible. This is too high a price to pay for reckoning with what ethnoscience has taught us. We must grant without prejudice that what other cultures and other times have produced as science differs from our own; we also argue with one another about whether science or, say, phenomenology, provides the better approach to experience. But when we are trying to create a theory of discourse, such concerns must be secondary to the conventions of discourse in our culture now. Our theory must be useful, isolating and describing kinds of discourses habitually distinguished by educated people in this time and place. My contention is that the notion of scientific discourse I have advanced more nearly achieves this goal; that Kinneavy has, in fact, described the conventions of "normal science" anyway; and that, by taking the publications of normal science as scientific discourse, we can at least test what Kinneavy and others have said about scientific discourse against a well-defined body of literature commonly recognized as indisputably scientific.

Exploratory and Expressive Discourse. Contemporary rhetoric has had a hard time with the concept of exploratory discourse. In *Rhetoric: Discovery and Change* (Young, Becker, and Pike), it wants on the one hand to substitute an open, exploratory rhetoric for the classical, agonistic model (8). On the other hand, it wants to subsume exploration to expression, as Britton comes close to doing (88), and Fulkerson seems inclined to do in his comments on the status of first drafts (45). Clearly, expression and exploration are closely related, as Kinneavy suggests in saying that of all types of reference discourse, exploration tolerates the greatest presence of expressive ingredients (188); however, Kinneavy also offers fairly sharp and clear distinctions between the two, which, if taken seriously, would largely clear up the conceptual confusion surrounding the two aims.

Kinneavy sees expressive discourse as the articulation of an individual or group's world—*world* in the sense of "life world," the existential world of immediate experience, the world of values, beliefs, and intensely personal feeling, not the abstract objective world that science attempts to describe, explain, and control. It would include, therefore, documents such as diaries, oaths and creeds, declarations and manifestos, notebooks of introspective jottings, records of dreams, and the like. Its stress on the encoder, on my world or our world (in the sense of group expression) makes it fundamentally different from exploration, which is turned toward *the* world, toward objects and processes distanced from subjectivity.

Exploration begins historically as dialectic in the sense of dialogue, its great exemplar being, of course, Plato. In Plato, as in all dialogue, one encounters personality and strongly held values and beliefs; however, the end of dialogue is not to articulate one's world but to scrutinize one's articulations. That is, dialectic may begin with expression, but its examination of assertions distances what is said from the encoder, making what I say an object of attention in itself. Though a sine qua non, expression itself is not the value of dialogue; the end of this oral form of exploratory discourse is, rather, the examined life—the objectivized life—consisting only of those assertions that can withstand the critique of others.

No value judgment is implied here: I am merely pointing to the central difference between expressive and exploratory discourse and suggesting that there is good reason to allot, as Kinneavy does, the former to the encoder, the latter to a subcategory of reference discourse.

Perhaps now we can see in part why expressive and exploratory discourse are often confused. Both are strongly oral; expression is the typical aim of conversation, most casual intercourse, as Edward Sapir pointed out (10–11); exploratory discourse is carried on most often and most felicitously in face-to-face dialogue. It is a short step from self-expression to self-examination; we will often find the two in tandem. Finally, there is the constant temptation first to equate exploration with self-exploration, as our inward-turned intellectual climate almost requires, and then to equate self-expression with expression. To do that, however, is to forget that anything can be explored and that exploratory discourse is ultimately interested in the self and its life world per se not as a source of intrinsic value but as the source of opinions for scrutiny.

When we turn from dialectical exploration to scientific exploration, the distinction between expressive and exploratory discourse becomes quite sharp, and the concentration of exploratory discourse on the object world of reference discourse becomes obvious. No one would confuse, say, Einstein's hypothetical papers on relativity or Chomsky's theoretical constructs with expressive discourse. Though by comparison more expressive, dialectic likewise should be distinguished from expressive discourse, for, like scientific exploration, it is looking for objectively valid generalizations. Dialectic and science share the exploratory aim; they differ in their choice of subject matter and method.

With the distinctions between expressive discourse and exploratory discourse in mind, we can better handle certain related problems, such as Fulkerson's query about the status of first drafts in Kinneavy's typology. Since Kinneavy explicitly excludes compositional process from his theory, he is not obliged to account for first drafts at all, but we have a legitimate interest in their theoretical status, especially in whether they should be considered expressive or exploratory.

The vast majority of first drafts are no more than stabs at one of the aims of discourse; as such, they present roughly the same classificatory problems as finished discourses. Some few drafts are of the sort we characterize by a statement like "I wrote this one for me" or "I just wanted to see what I think." Such drafts sound expressive, and indeed they are. But then all discourse, as Kinneavy says, is expressive; expression is "psychologically prior" because nothing gets said or written unless somebody wants or needs to do so (396). And even a grocery list is self-revealing. To say, however, that see-what-I-think drafts are expressive is about as helpful as saying that all discourse is suasive in some sense, if only as "I" appealing to "me"; both statements are true, but irrelevant to the question of classification.

Clearly, we must distinguish for typological purposes, as Kinneavy does implicitly, between expression and expressive discourse. If "I wrote this for me" means "I wrote this about me, my life world, my identity, and my identifications," then we can say that the draft is expressive discourse. But if it means, "I wrote this to analyze my beliefs and values, to examine more closely using the discipline of writing my casual thoughts on a particular subject," I can imagine no other category but exploratory discourse for such a draft.

If at least some of the see-what-I-think drafts are exploratory, then we must hold that there is such a thing as genuinely exploratory written discourse. However, after Ong's work on the psychology of print, one can see why few instances of printed exploration exist. Our written exploratory drafts are almost always published only in the sense of being read by a few trusted colleagues. They don't often appear in print because the medium calls for closure, not open-endedness. Even writing is uneasy with exploration as an end in itself; exploratory first drafts normally are bridges to something else. And scientific exploration normally represses much of its oral, dialectical origin, giving the impression of conclusiveness that well-trained scientists, in unguarded moments, seem to take as conclusive, as fact rather than theory. There is, then, a kind of cultural enmity between print and exploration; the few genuine instances of printed exploration that are not just first drafts often turn out to be draftlike after all, such as Wittgenstein's *Philosophical Investigations*.

The Other Aims. The two remaining types of discourse, informative and literary, have received little serious criticism, and I have but a few points to make about them myself at this juncture.

From the standpoint of composition pedagogy, probably the most significant distinction Kinneavy makes is that between informative and persuasive discourse, too often before him collapsed into the single category, exposition. Discarding the term *exposition* altogether, he develops informative discourse in a way that should help to end the still persistent confusion of information with persuasion. For example, informative discourse must tell us something new (at least new for us, the audience or readership);

persuasion draws on strongly rooted belief, on the old, on matters thought to be known so well that the rhetorical tradition calls them commonplaces. Informative discourse must give us all relevant knowledge about the topics as defined and restricted by the author, but no one expects a persuasive work to be comprehensive in this sense. Typically, persuasion is selective, using what is known only as it helps in the proving of contentions. Bias, of course, is always present in informative discourse; however, obvious bias renders the aim, as the speech-act theorists might say, infelicitous, whereas bias in persuasion is taken for granted.

The norms Kinneavy describes are highly significant culturally; the difference between persuasion and information is supposed to set a news story apart from news commentary and editorializing, for instance. Clearly, our students must learn these norms, if only to be critical of them. It is therefore a misplaced criticism to contend, as Fulkerson does, that Kinneavy confuses the normative and the descriptive in his treatment of informative discourse (44–45). In the first place, all description has a normative aspect, if only in the choice of an example to describe. In the second place, as teachers and critics we have to provide norms—the very concept of aim implies something to shoot for, a target that will allow us to evaluate a writer's aim. A theory is by nature normative: one may dispute the norms Kinneavy attributes to informative discourse, but not the normative urge itself.

The problem of norm is especially acute in literary discourse, the serious playfulness of which routinely results in the deliberate fracturing of conventions. With literature in the narrow sense of *poesis*, there is a prior or higher theoretical problem, one that none of our theorists address—whether literature is properly a form of discourse at all. One could very well answer that it is not, that literature ought to be considered in the same general category with painting, sculpture, music, dance. That, in fact, is how philosophy since Kant has generally regarded literature, as a special case of language use and therefore exempt from the kind of evaluation one applies to discourse that purports to make statements about the objective world. Viewed in this way, literature is a problem for aesthetics, not for a theory of discourse.

Obviously, we cannot evaluate anyone's treatment of literature as discourse until we decide whether literature is discourse. I postpone the consideration of this issue, however, until we consider Moffett's theory, since the problems of literature's place emerge most sharply there. We can say that Kinneavy's view of literature is too formalistic as gauged by present theoretical norms. If we want to claim literature as a form of discourse, we cannot do so by full acceptance of Kinneavy's emphasis on literature as objects of art; such a view moves us toward literature as a fine art and not as a type of discourse. In the Moffett chapter, we will pursue these issues in greater depth.

The Modes

Kinneavy's modes are much harder to evaluate than his aims. Kinneavy himself seems diffident about them: whereas he claims that any instance of discourse will fall within one or a combination of his aims, he makes no such claim to exhaustiveness for the modes (Kinneavy et al., *Modes* 10). Here is my list, he says, but there may be more.

Perhaps dissatisfaction with the modes accounts partly for his never having produced the second volume of *Theory*, which was to deal with the modes at length. His fullest account of them so far is in *Writing: Basic Modes of Organization*, on which the following discussion is based.

Certain problems will likely beset any theory of discourse modes. Even though Kinneavy grounds them both philosophically and historically, he does not entirely escape the sense of arbitrariness surrounding modality in general. For instance, the mode of classification subsumes definition, comparison and contrast, analogy, and the like, often discriminated in rhetoric texts as distinct modes in themselves. Obviously, this grouping is related somehow, but which among them is the basic mode? One could argue that definition (in the sense of genus or species) makes explicit what is only implicit in acts of classification, so that classification would precede definition because one must have already classified before one can define. Perhaps, then, classification is the basic mode here. To classify, however, one must detect likeness among objects or processes not identical. Analogy seems "more basic" in the sense of both logical and temporal priority; it must come before both definition and classification. Kinneavy's decision to treat classification as basic, and definition, comparison and contrast, analogy, and so on, as subdivisions, seems purely arbitrary.

Also arbitrary is Kinneavy's limiting of the modes to four basic ones. While Kinneavy's modes certainly have an explicit rationale (as, for example, Alexander Bain's forms of discourse do not), one may have serious doubts about the rationale itself. Why, for example, out of all the conceptual contrasts in Western philosophy, should we limit ourselves to being/becoming, essence/existence, and potency/act as a basis for modal discrimination? Perelman lists fourteen such conceptual contrasts as typical of philosophical inquiry (420); why not use some of these? And why rely on the status theory identified with Cicero and legal rhetoric as a model for modality in discourse generally?

To see the problem more concretely, let us consider the status of arguments. An argument is clearly not an aim. Though we say, So-and-so argues just to argue, argument really pursues some end—to inquire (exploratory discourse), to win assent from an audience (persuasion), perhaps to vent hostility in the form of pointless contentiousness (expression), or to demonstrate the probable truth of a hypothesis (science). Argument, or more precisely the mimesis of argument, turns up in literature as well, as in Swift's "Modest Proposal." About the only aim argument does not subserve is informative discourse. What, then, is it, if not a mode? Kinneavy says the modes are a means of organization. What more common way of organizing a discourse than by argument, by case structure?

While obviously there would be mnemonic advantages to a short list of modes, such a consideration has no theoretical standing, nor does Kinneavy defend his four on that basis. On the grounds just offered, I would hold that argument should also be a mode, and doubtless others could be advanced with philosophical or historical justification behind them. In short, not only are the subdivisions of the modes arbitrary, but also ultimately the list of four itself is arbitrary.

Another difficulty connected with any modal theory is that modes tend to merge insensibly with topics of invention. Kinneavy treats definition, for instance, as part of the mode of classification, while Aristotle put it in his list of topoi. Because invention and arrangement are "Siamese twins" (Knapp), a category like definition has always a double aspect: on the one hand, it is a means of organization, as when one begins a discourse by defining terms used in a special way; on the other, it is a means of generating content. Kinneavy realizes the dual function of his modes: in one place he says that "more than any other aspect of composition, modes determine organization" (Modes 4); in another, he calls the modes "windows on reality" (Modes 9), implying heuristic value. But it is not clear whether Kinneavy means to substitute his modes for the traditional topics or how the modes relate to the topics if they are somehow distinguishable. The result is confusion.

Another source of difficulty is Kinneavy's understanding of the modes. Unlike the aims of discourse, which designate purposes intrinsic to discourse, the modes are connected with the vexing philosophical problem of reference, of how words and propositions manage to connect meaningfully with nonverbal objects and processes. Kinneavy believes that "the ultimate attempt of discourse to refer to reality should, as much as possible, be grounded in the nature of reality, not the nature of language" (Theory 36). That is why he grounds his modes "in certain philosophical concepts of the nature of reality considered as being and becoming," and not in concepts about language or discourse per se.

Since, for example, description attempts to isolate something and discuss its features, clearly a theory of modes depends on a theory of reference. We not only lack a theory of reference, but we must also reckon with formidable current arguments to the effect that language is nonreferential. If there is a solution to the problem of reference, I have no idea what it is. It seems certain, however, that one cannot separate the nature of reality from the nature of language. Reality itself is a concept and therefore linguistic, and language itself evolves within concrete cultural and material contexts, part of reality as humans necessarily experience it. We cannot hope, therefore, to ground modes "in the nature of reality" as opposed to "the nature of language" even "as much as possible," for it is clearly impossible. If we conceive the modes as Kinneavy did, we will begin by posing the problem in a way that makes a solution unobtainable.

All in all, it is fair to say that Kinneavy's modes are considerably less successful as a theoretical construct than his aims are. This is so in part because the modes involve greater, perhaps even insuperable, problems and in part because of the way in which Kinneavy conceives the modes. I am saying, then, that the whole notion of mode must be rethought.

In saying that the modes must be rethought, I am obviously implying that the concept itself has value and ought to be retained in any synthesis of discourse theory. Basically, Kinneavy's modal concept serves a bridging function. On the one hand, we have the process of writing, dominated by invention and especially by various traditional and contemporary topoi. On the other hand, we have the products of writing, the features of finished discourses, Kinneavy's main preoccupation. Indisputably, that which is re-covered, uncovered, or discovered in invention does not leap magically untransformed into the final product but undergoes much shaping and reshaping; there are choices and resulting structures that mediate between discovery and final version and eventuate in the preproduct products of our tentative drafts. Of course, many of our decisions are the result of aim and audience considerations and thus have nothing directly to do with modes per se. But whatever topoi we consciously or unconsciously use must even-tuate in something, in some structure or another more or less recognizable on a page. These structures or means of development are the modes. They turn up in the process as soon as we write anything toward a preliminary draft, and they are what we rework in our struggle to achieve a satisfactory final text. Hence, the modes are mediatory or bridging; they are the link between prewriting and writing, observable in the final product and in the drafts on the way to the final product.

However inadequate Kinneavy's discussion of the modes may be, he has given us a valuable concept that cannot simply be discarded because of initial misconception or such an apparently permanent quandary as the problem of reference.

Conclusion

Kenneth Burke once stoically remarked that anything written or said can be praised for what it hits or condemned for what it misses. Kinneavy's theory has suffered both fates. I should now like to put my own criticisms of *A Theory of Discourse* in perspective as part of an overall assessment.

On the whole, my reservations are reservations of detail. I disagree with Kinneavy's effort to objectify aim, seeing it rather as a judgment made about a text or about a writer's motives somewhere in the process of writing. But I have no doubts about the value of the aim concept itself. Similarly, for many reasons, I want to confine the scientific aim to narrower parameters than Kinneavy does, but I have no doubt that there is such an aim that can be distinguished from the others. I find both the number and the internal organization of the modes problematical, but I have no argument with the value of the concept itself and nothing but praise for Kinneavy's effort to ground modes philosophically and historically. We ought not to rest content with a mere ad hoc modal list.

Where I do differ from Kinneavy on fundamental points, my position should not be construed as a wholesale rejection of his theory. I agree with Fulkerson that Kinneavy's deterministic view of aim must be discounted. But, as Fulkerson points out, Kinneavy himself retreats from this hypothesis within *Theory* itself (49). Implicitly, Kinneavy has a multidimensional view, which, with Britton's help, we can exploit more fully.

Another fundamental difference between my view of discourse and Kinneavy's in *Theory* is the significance that I, and practically everyone else in modern rhetoric, attach to writing as a process. When Kinneavy chose early in *Theory* not to pursue the process implications of the term *composition*, he opted for half a theory at best. What he gave us amounts to a static model of adult-level competence, a theory that articulates the kinds of discourse within which an ideally mature writer ought to be able to perform. Such a model is invaluable for the teaching of writing, because it gives us a sense of ultimate goals, the "what" to which our continual involvement with discourse processes ought always to be headed. However, apart from his concern with the history of discourse instruction and discourse types, he sheds little light on any of the other meanings of process in discourse— process in the sense of the act of composing or in the development of discourse ability, for example. In short, Kinneavy tells us where we want to go but not how to get there; that is what I mean by saying he gave us half a theory. The other half—the process half—we must seek in Britton, Moffett, and D'Angelo.

A Theory of Discourse, then, is not adequate in itself; it demands its complement, the process dimension, as surely as product implies process (and vice versa). This said, however, no evaluation of Kinneavy would be fair or complete if we neglected what he did achieve, which includes many contributions besides his discourse typology. In the long run I suspect we will appreciate more than we have thus far the historical awareness Kinneavy brought to the theoretical task, a profound sense of tradition not shared notably by our other three theorists. Wherever Kinneavy works, he works consciously in a matrix of past thought and discourse praxis, which gives his theory a special resonance and depth. For reasons too numerous and complicated to discuss here, modern rhetoric is in constant danger of either forgetting its heritage altogether or turning that heritage into a mere relic of antiquarian interest. In both *Theory* and his subsequent freshman text, *Writing in the Liberal Arts Tradition* (Kinneavy, McCleary, and Nakadate), Kinneavy situates composition in the tradition of classical education in a vital and functional way. Doubtless we will appropriate aspects of the tradition that Kinneavy ignored or barely touched; doubtless we will interpret the past in ways quite different from his. Without serious impoverishment, however, we cannot theorize effectively by attending only to our admittedly urgent present problems. Here, as elsewhere, Kinneavy exemplifies thinking we must eventually undertake ourselves if the revival of rhetoric in English departments is to achieve a fuller self-understanding.

Part of this thinking has been, and must be, about the field of English itself. Kinneavy's contribution is twofold. First, his theory systematically justifies much of what we have been doing in English departments all along. Even the most conservative, literature-oriented department has in fact been studying and teaching much more than *poesis* proper. For example, standard literature courses offer both the *Lyrical Ballads* and the "Preface" to that volume, the latter being, of course, not *poesis* but a combination of expressive and persuasive discourse. Even the staunchest purist is really no purist at all. Such an angle of vision puts the perennial conflicts between rhetorician and literary critic in better perspective, suggesting that the enemy the critic would keep outside the castle of culture is actually manning the battlements.

Second, while leading us despite ourselves to a better understanding of what we have always done, Kinneavy's theory also justifies the broadening of English studies over the last twenty years or so in less traditional departments. Business and technical writing, for instance, finds its place in referential and persuasive discourse.

As significant as it is, however, Kinneavy's comprehensive view of English is much more than a systematic justification of the field. It is ultimately a call for reform as well as an understanding of what presently exists. Kinneavy's theory, for example, does not sanction the privileged position that traditional literary study still holds. Literature is simply one of four aims in a nonhierarchical view of discourse purposes. Literature has, in Kinneavy's view, a distinctive nature and value, but its nature and value are not intrinsically better than any of the other aims. It follows that Kinneavy's ideal department would not be disproportionately staffed by literary scholars; instead of being English in the sense of literature in English with ancillary disciplines barely tolerated on the fringes, it would be English in the sense of the language and its discourse. The student of scientific discourse or persuasive discourse would have equal footing.

Such a department would also have to renew interest in areas of study long ceded to other departments. For instance, the serious study of logic, now primarily the concern of philosophy, would be a legitimate area of specialization in English as well, though confined mainly to the logic of natural language or the logics of the various discourse aims and modes.

In sum, Kinneavy's challenge, issuing from a total theoretical vision that no one else holding similar views can claim, is twofold: to remake English departments so that they will be truly concerned with English, that is, the language and all its uses; and to reverse the fragmentation of English, which began when speech went its own way, followed by linguistics, and now, in some places, by rhetoric. Since one can hardly study the written apart from the oral, or discourse without an understanding of the language, or compositions apart from composing, surely the reintegration of English always implicit and sometimes explicit in Kinneavy's theory must be achieved somehow, even if, as seems likely, nothing can be done about the slow dismemberment of our field into ever smaller bureaucratic units.

Ultimately, an understanding of Kinneavy amounts to a sharing of his total theoretical vision of English, because his attempt to order the past meaningfully for the present, to comprehend what we are, and to project toward what we might be are all of a piece and function as the context of his discourse theory. While this sharing need not imply total agreement in general, much less in detail, it can nevertheless reveal why E. P. J. Corbett called *A Theory of Discourse* "one of the truly important works of our time." In scope, depth, and simultaneous concern with detail and integration, it still has no rival, remaining indisputably at the center of our thought about the universe of discourse.

CHAPTER TWO

MOFFETT'S THEORY

Overview

James Moffett's *Teaching the Universe of Discourse* attempts to correlate child development with interrelations among discourse types, to discover a "proper learning order" by "looking for the main lines of child development and to assimilate to them, when fitting, the various formulations that scholars make about language and literature" (14).

Although Moffett, like Kinneavy, grounds his theory in the communication triangle, he discriminates discourses not by aim but by "shifts in the relations among persons—increasing rhetorical distance between speaker and listener, and increasing abstractive altitude between the raw subject matter of some subject and the speaker's symbolization of it" (10).

"Increasing rhetorical distance between speaker and listener" is the I-you relation. It ranges from interior dialogue through conversation and correspondence to publication. Developmentally, interior dialogue derives from the vocalizations that so often accompany the acts of young children; Piaget calls this dialogue "egocentric speech," since it is not addressed to others (32). The suppression of egocentric speech yields true interior dialogue, sometimes called intrapersonal communication—the verbal dimension of thought itself. Next removed from the inner voice is conversation, wherein *I* achieves greater distance from *you* because speaker and auditor are no longer within the same nervous system. From conversation we move to writing, to correspondence, nonoral because the communicants are now separate from each other in space. Finally there is publication, impersonal, with author and reader often widely separated in both space and time.

A learner's ability to discourse at the various levels along the I-you dimension is determined by a host of environmental and genetic factors. Moffett relates mature communication to the developmental ability to de-

center and abstract, concepts so closely related as to be almost indistinguishable. Decentering conceives a self speaking to another self whose
interest and values may be very different; we speak to our *construct* of this
other self, to an abstraction from our total experience with our interlocutor.
Compared with the impersonal publication audience, the "other" of conversation is relatively concrete, perceived through the formulated and tacit
knowledge garnered from face-to-face contact.

The writer typically has no such contact, has in fact no audience but
rather a readership, which is, according to Walter Ong, a fiction, only
distantly and vaguely connected to actual individuals ("Writer's Audience"
60–61). The mature communicator, therefore, must decenter and abstract
to a far greater degree to write than to converse, perhaps a developmental
explanation for the priority of conversation.

Moffett also bases his discussion of the I-it dimension, the relation of
speaker or writer to material or subject matter, on a scale of abstraction.
The lowest (nearest to raw phenomenon) is *recording*, an account of *what is
happening*. Recording is abstract because of the selectivity of perception:
what is seen and heard is conditioned by prior experience, by what we
expect to encounter. Still more abstract is *reporting*, an account of *what has
happened*: it depends on the selectivity of memory as well as perception.
Recording and reporting, while abstract, relate directly to concrete hap-
penings. *Generalizing*, the next level of abstracting, takes a number of re-
corded or reported events and treats them as sufficiently alike to permit an
account of *what happens*. Generalizing's mode is analogic rather than chronologic, and concrete events in their particularity retreat in favor of interpretation. Finally, on the basis of our understanding of what happens, we
speculate about *what may happen*; that is, we theorize. *Theorizing* attempts
to synthesize into one coherent, explanatory, predictive view many judgments about what happens. Theories are essentially inferences from prior
generalizations, purely verbal in the sense that they are statements about
statements. The theoretical mode, therefore, based on generalizations rooted
in records and reports, is predominantly tautological.

In sum, as we move from recording to theorizing along the I-it dimension,
we move from discourse close to the structure of the phenomenal world
to discourse close to the structure of language itself—closer, one assumes,
to the structure of mind.

To complete Moffett's general picture of the universe of discourse, we
should survey the discourse types in relation to the I-you and I-it dimensions. *What is happening* includes the on-the-scene verbalizing so familiar
from radio, television news, notes taken during meetings. But beyond these
quotidian senses of recording, what is happening embraces interior dialogue,

dialogue, and drama—all forms of discourse, so to speak, in the present tense.

What has happened, retrospective construction, includes such familiar genres as minutes, letters, diaries, journals, autobiography, memoirs, chronicles, and history, as well as most fiction. Note that audiences range from the personal to the impersonal, from self-directed, as in some diaries, to fictive, as in written histories and novels.

Generalizing and theorizing, though a part of mature thought and conversation, are the special domain of science and philosophy, of systematic inquiry, organized bodies of knowledge, critiques, and metacritiques, and thus include such forms as the essay, the tract, and the journal article.

Analysis

One could hardly create a theory more antithetical to Kinneavy's than that of Moffett. Whereas Kinneavy abstracts discourse from process in all the meanings of process except the history of discourse, Moffett grounds his theory in process as the development of discourse ability vis-à-vis general intellectual growth. Kinneavy seeks, above all, a stable and fixed concept of aim and a typology of aims that would sharply discriminate means from ends in discourse; Moffett's thrust is not so much toward conceptual clarity as toward a learning sequence, the nature of which pushes us beyond categorical thought, toward seeing the more concrete relations among discourse kinds. This difference in motive probably also accounts for their contrasting spirits: Kinneavy is authoritative in attitude and method, whereas Moffett freely admits that his "is not a completely systematic and consistent theory, but rather a central way of thinking" (211).

I perceive Moffett to be the counterstatement to Kinneavy's statement. In the first half of the following analysis, I bring out the consequences of Moffett's way of thinking by comparison with Kinneavy's. In calling Moffett the counterstatement to Kinneavy's statement, I do not mean to imply that Moffett's work is in any way dependent on Kinneavy or that it is less valuable. Quite the contrary: I see Moffett's theory as in many respects more advanced than Kinneavy's even though *Teaching the Universe of Discourse* antedates *A Theory of Discourse* by three years. My reason for the thesis-antithesis view of Kinneavy and Moffett is that they seem to represent the major alternatives of modern thought in rhetoric and composition. While I want to make these alternatives as understandable as possible, I suggest that the kinds of thought their respective theories embody are not really alternatives but ultimately complements.

Basic Assumptions

Moffett presents us with an apparently flat choice between two starting points: either we proceed as he does by "looking for the main lines of child development and assimilating to them, when fitting, the various formulations that scholars make about language and literature," or we begin "with some notions of structure derived from linguistics or literary criticism and try to found a curriculum on them by negotiating a compromise between theory and the classroom facts of life" (14). Although Kinneavy was after a theory of discourse per se and not a theory to guide curricular sequences, the second way is clearly his way. Thus, we have divergent goals and sharply opposing assumptions about where to start. The advantage may appear to lie with Moffett. Why negotiate a compromise between theory and practice when one can begin with "the classroom facts of life"? Unfortunately, the choice is not so appealingly simple or clear as Moffett makes it sound.

The choice, for instance, is not between fact and theory; discovering the main lines of child development is itself a heavily theory-laden enterprise, as Moffett recognizes when he points to the hypothetical nature of Piaget's notion of decentering (57). In establishing "a proper learning order," theories from developmental psychology will surely be more relevant than "the various formulations that scholars make about language and literature" (14), but no less theoretical.

What does "classroom facts of life" mean, anyway? Moffett does not elaborate, so one must take him to mean the relative level of cognitive development and general maturity of a class as a whole as well as individuals in the class. But surely the facts come to much more than cognitive development and maturity, taking in a whole realm of tacit knowledge derived from praxis itself, day-to-day involvement with a specific group in a specific time and place. If so, there will always be a need to negotiate a compromise between theory and the classroom facts of life, no matter what conceptual base one starts from.

Moffett's claim to a privileged theoretical approach may be justified, but not on the grounds he adduced. His claim is no less theoretical or more concrete than Kinneavy's. (Indeed, when one recalls the minute analysis of discourse in Kinneavy, a kind of concreteness altogether absent from Moffett, one might well conclude that Kinneavy is less abstract.) Neither is very close to the classroom facts of life, which include such grim realities as underfed children and underprepared teachers. Nor is Moffett's approach more relevant even in an absolute sense; if one happens to be teaching older or more talented students, Kinneavy's static model of adult-level competence may seem more to the point than any developmental view.

In short, Moffett's special claim to our attention is not lodged in any innate superiority of theoretical approach. Rather, it is in the urgency of the question he addresses: What constitutes a proper learning order? There is just no other question more important—and more resistant to a definitive answer—than this one.

The Idea of a Learning Sequence

Without an overall picture of how discourse competence develops, no English curriculum can claim a firm foundation. As Moffett points out, a curriculum must be more than logical; it must be psychological as well—in step with where the students are. And this demand, at least on the face of it, does not seem impracticable; if we can discover the general order in which children acquire a mature syntax, can we not uncover the order of discourse acquisition? The notion of a learning sequence, however, is highly problematical, both in itself and in relation to discourse theory. We cannot assess Moffett's contribution apart from understanding what the question itself involves.

To begin with, theory can articulate only the idea of a learning sequence and any hypotheses about it. Establishing such a sequence, if there is one, requires extensive empirical research. Unfortunately, the problem is not just one of time and money to collect and analyze student scripts at age or grade levels or to follow individual students as they develop. Rather, it is that there are just too many variables that influence discourse competence. Unlike speech, writing is clearly not innate, implicit in the genes, so to speak. As a technology with a cultural base, writing depends on a host of fluctuating attitudes and values, making the interpretation of empirical data very difficult. Furthermore, discourse competence is not separable from general intellectual growth; we must correlate whatever we discover about the development of writing ability with, for example, research in cognition.

What is Moffett's contribution to the establishment of a learning sequence? We may credit him with bringing the question itself to the fore but not, of course, with the basic idea of a learning sequence, which is at least as old as ancient Greek education. And while Moffett helps us to see the relevance of Piaget's theories for our particular problems, the basic hypotheses of *Teaching the Universe of Discourse* are Piaget's, not Moffett's. Nor does Moffett contribute anything to the empirical end of establishing a learning sequence, though he goes on in a later book to shape a whole curriculum around his vision of it.

Moffett's real contribution is a revolutionary way of thinking about discourse that cuts across both traditional theory and the departmental divisions of modern educational practice. He shows us how to think about discourse in developmental, rather than merely categorical, terms. We may be no nearer to a reliable learning sequence at the end of his book, but we have participated in the kind of thought that might eventually lead to one.

Use of the Triangle

In "A Pluralistic Synthesis of Four Contemporary Models for Teaching Composition," Kinneavy points out that the communication triangle is common to all four of our theories (38). This is true, but to say that both he and Moffett use the triangle is roughly the equivalent of saying that Hegel and Marx were both dialecticians. It conceals much more than it reveals, for the specific way Moffett uses the triangle is almost diametrically opposed to Kinneavy's way. We can begin to appreciate how Moffett would have us think about discourse by contrasting the function of the triangle in his theory with its function in Kinneavy.

Ever since Aristotle distinguished three kinds of persuasive discourse, the dominant mode of rhetorical thought has been categorical. That is, faced with a universe of discourse, we have sought to comprehend it in part by some sort of classificatory scheme. The implicit principle at work is well put by Britton: "writing cannot be regarded globally" (3). Most of the good in good writing is so only in relation to a particular kind of discourse. The ends of the epideictic orator are not the same as those of the forensic speaker; what is appropriate for expressive discourse usually will not be appropriate for scientific discourse.

As the latter example suggests, Kinneavy is mainstream traditional in seeking first and foremost typologies with which to order the domain of discourse. He finds problems with some past concepts used for this purpose, but he never questions the value of categorical thought itself. Nor should we if we agree with Britton's principle. At the same time, we cannot afford to overlook the limitations of categorical thought, either. The main limitation is not that typologies inevitably leak, failing to provide a clean-cut place for some of the phenomena they would classify. Such limitation is simply endemic to all concepts; we will just have to live with it. Rather, the main limitation is a one-sided dialectic, a tendency to obscure relations and interrelations in the very act of making useful distinctions, a tendency to reify the concept to the point at which its seemingly fixed and stable nature begins to cover over the shifting identities of a phenomenal world always in process.

Kinneavy makes two central moves early in *A Theory of Discourse*: first, he chooses not to feature the term *composition* on the grounds that its process implications run counter to his purpose, a typology of discourse products; second, and more important within our present focus, having derived the communication triangle from the structure of the communicative act, he introduces the notion of foregrounding, the hypothesis that most discourse can be classified according to the element or point on the triangle it emphasizes—the addressor, the addressee, and so on. It is this move that leads directly to the central concept of aim and thence to Kinneavy's typology of aims. One can say that Kinneavy's theory is completely dependent on—even perhaps deducible from—these two opening moves; they are key to both his strengths and his weaknesses.

Moffett's gambit, if you will, consists in making almost exactly the opposite moves. Instead of turning away from process, he emphasizes it in at least two senses: as the development of discourse abilities and as the teaching of discourse by discoursing. Consequently, he has no interest in a systematic discourse typology; he is quite content to place conventional genres (autobiography, history, personal letter, etc.) with respect to his scales of abstraction. Contrary to the notion of foregrounding, which inevitably leads us to think by dissociation (e.g., the addressor apart from the addressee, expressive discourse as contrasted with persuasion), Moffett deals with the basic structure of someone talking to somebody about something much more concretely, closer to what it really is in the act of composing, in the I-you and I-it relations. In this way, Moffett gives voice to the other side of the dialectic connected with the triangle: if the addressor and the addressee are distinct and can be treated apart from each other, as Kinneavy perceives them, they are also merged in the sense that the "I," the writer, must contain the "other," creating that persona when fictionalizing a readership.

What Moffett does both here and almost everywhere in *Teaching the Universe of Discourse* is break through the limitations of categorical thought. No more or less than Kinneavy, Moffett must use categories; a category, after all, is only a more rigorous and conceptually explicit version of the basic language function of naming. As such, it is both enabling and disabling. It enables Kinneavy, for example, to distinguish reference discourse from persuasion and to subdivide reference discourse into three other categories, a vast improvement over the lumping of nearly everything except creative writing under the catch-all term *exposition*. But it also disables or limits Kinneavy's thought about discourse in two main ways: first, categorical thought per se results in a set of rubrics under which examples are classified in laundry-list fashion; second, in sharply setting this against that, it obscures the relations and interrelations among the kinds distinguished so that moving without hiatus from one type of discourse to another becomes virtually impossible.

Clearly Moffett's thought overcomes the more negative consequences of thinking in categories. Moffett gives us no laundry lists, no mere enumeration of examples or illustrative types; instead, employing the relations in the triangle, he leads us to see types of discourse in linked sequences. Where Kinneavy isolates narrative from his other modes and cites varieties of narration in no particular order and as illustrations only, Moffett devotes a long and fascinating chapter to the same mode, leaving us with a total vision of it, beginning with narratives close to concrete, personal experience (e.g., diaries, journals, personal letters) and ending with the abstract, impersonal narratives of history, science, and philosophy. Where Kinneavy leads us to see, perhaps, a personal letter and a history as unrelated, as types of discourse belonging to different aims (presumably expression and reference, respectively), Moffett shows us how to perceive history through the personal letter, part of the raw data that history digests in constructing its more impersonal accounts of what happened.

Moffett's undermining of static abstraction by dynamic modes of thought is scarcely restricted to the communication triangle. Indeed, his dissolving of categorical thought manifests itself throughout *Teaching the Universe of Discourse*. Let us turn now to some of its other manifestations.

The Field of English

Regardless of what the educational establishment might say about English, they treat the field as if it were just one subject among others in the daily round of classes; students take English as they take speech or math or history or science. And English itself is a hodge-podge, a little literature, a little grammar, a little writing, a little of this skill and that skill and not much of anything in particular. The description, alas, is all too familiar and very resistant to change.

In a manner that Aristotle would admire, Kinneavy brings conceptual clarity to the field of English, neatly dividing study of the language itself, linguistics, from study of its use, the field of discourse. Using the triangle, which systematically structures so much in *A Theory of Discourse*, he divides and subdivides each field into areas and subareas, producing an impressive example of what categorical thought can do. If taken seriously, his vision of the field of English might transform university English departments, but it leaves the major problems alluded to in the last paragraph untouched. Moffett, by contrast, confronts them head on, working away at the very pattern of thought that produces the featureless, flat monotony of so much contemporary education.

Whereas Moffett makes fluid discourse categories by stressing overlap and interrelation, here he tries to break through prevailing abstraction by reconceptualizing. English, he purports, is not a field, not a subject or area of study to be put casually on the same level with, for example, astronomy or American history. Rather, like math and mathlike artificial languages, English is a symbol system, the very medium by which we inquire, formulate, and communicate in all areas of study. Symbol systems are not primarily something one learns about; they are systems one learns to use. But the result of treating English as only a subject among other subjects is to confuse knowing about with knowing how, and the eclipse of the latter by the former. As Moffett says, the teaching of English has usually been "too substantive":

> Units on style, logic, and rhetoric can teach little more than abstract information if these things are not kept as functions of each other, and they can be kept so only in the ultimate context of somebody-talking-to-somebody-else-about-something. (5)

In short, language "is truly language only when it is being used" (118). Our students do not "know" English simply by virtue of being able to enunciate grammatical principles or recite facts about this or that author; they know English when they can play the whole symbolic scale, speaking, reading, and writing effectively through the whole range of the I-it and I-you relationships, and when they know where they are on the scale at any given time.

Moffett's reconceptualization of the field of English is truly radical in its implications; it strikes at the roots of contemporary education. Typically, we contrast the verbal with the quantitative, linking the verbal with the liberal arts, the quantitative with science and its technological applications. While this cut can be justified, it obscures Moffett's more fundamental slicing—the division of symbol systems from content subjects, from the use of languages, natural and artificial, for talking about some aspect or portion of the phenomenal world. If we make the cut where Moffett makes it, we cannot justify treating English as just one of many subjects in a curriculum. Nor can we think of English itself along Kinneavy's lines, as only a discipline consisting of so many subdisciplines, each with its special focus, just like any other field. English becomes *the* basic, since all learning takes the form of discourse; English itself transforms from a conglomeration of courses in language, composition, and literature to a curriculum wherein all "knowing about" arises in the context of actual discoursing, of learning how. The piecemeal, unit approach, a typical outcome of categorical thought, gives way to Moffett's functional, organic approach and to a classroom that generally eschews the lecture format of content subjects in favor of maximum action and interaction with language.

Furthermore, from Moffett's perspective the content subjects themselves look different. Our students take history, science, and philosophy, for example, without any concept of how these disciplines relate to one another, as if the differences between them were only differences in subject matter. (This is what I meant when I referred earlier in this section to the flat monotony of a round of course work.) But if all fields must use discourse, we can distinguish and relate them by how they use the powers of language. Here again, Kinneavy's categorical distinctions do not help, for the discourse of all content subjects is for Kinneavy just so much reference discourse. Moffett's dynamic view, however, at least sheds some light, allowing us to see the content subjects by degree of abstractive altitude.

Consider, for example, history and science. The former is certainly abstract, purporting to tell us what happened by drawing inferences from whatever remains of the documents of an age, these documents themselves standing at several removes from raw experience and reflecting the biases of perception, memory, and interest. History is, then, a summary of summaries, an interpretation of interpretations. It is by no means as concrete a subject as it may seem; often much of the record has been lost and the historian cannot know all of what remains or escape the limitations of available source material and of personal bias, especially the factor of interest.

But if history amounts to a high-level abstraction, science is higher still; if history offers an account of unique events, science discovers what is common to a class of events. History tells us what happened; science aims not only at what happens (always and everywhere) but also, based on observation and experiment, at what may (or must) happen, striving for reliable prediction and, where possible, control of the future.

Of course, science's higher abstractive altitude in no way makes science better than history. Moffett's symbolic scale is designed not to evaluate the worth of the various fields of study but to help us reveal to our students how the subjects they study relate to world and to one another. The ultimate objective is to empower our students to think for themselves. Instead of moving unquestioningly from one class full of authoritative pronouncements to another class full of the same, as if there were empty heads to be filled with imperial gallons of hard facts, we can use Moffett to enable students to inquire—to ask, for example, why history must be continually rewritten, exactly how history itself differs from a philosophy or science of history, and how science is limited by its very power to abstract. Moffett's way is the way of education rather than indoctrination. To play the whole symbolic scale and to know where one is on it at any particular time is to be more fully human, to approach Plato's ancient ideal of a truly free person's education.

Orality and Literacy

The modern tendency of the humanities to ape the sciences, to divide and subdivide into ever smaller concentrations, has been much lamented by would-be reformers. No field has been more dismembered than English, which has undergone not only fragmentation but also alienation. Distinguished subareas of English have become separate departments—speech led the way, splitting from English near the turn of the century, followed at many large universities by linguistics, folklore, theater, journalism, and rhetoric. Despite efforts to counter this trend, strongly entrenched habits of mind join with powerful political and economic incentives to render any hope of genuine reunification very faint indeed.

Is English a Humpty-Dumpty? What can be done to liberate English from the narrow and quite possibly suicidal identification with literary studies only? Both Kinneavy and Moffett propose the same solution at one level—that English should encompass all discourse in the language, not just *poesis* proper. But Moffett is able to go one step beyond Kinneavy in drawing together the dissociated fragments of our field because he thinks of discourse developmentally, dynamically, rather than in Kinneavy's static, categorical terms. Specifically, what Moffett does is expose the unreality of turning the oral-literate distinction into a dichotomy and the havoc wrought in educational practice by departmentalizing speech, drama, and English, as if these vitally interconnected fields were really separate disciplines or courses of study.

Perhaps the best way to appreciate fully what Moffett's theoretical approach can accomplish is by contrasting it with Kinneavy's. Kinneavy certainly recognizes the oral-literate distinction: it is implicit in his treatment of arts and media (*Theory* 31) and alluded to in passing on numerous occasions. In essence Kinneavy works at a level of abstraction beyond the oral-literate distinction, his typology of aims being designed to classify discourses regardless of medium. For this reason he sheds little to no light on the issues raised by the oral-literate distinction, nor can he help us overcome the departmentalizing of the language arts. Furthermore, even if one proposed, as I have, to refine Kinneavy's aims by systematically distinguishing oral and literate forms ("Comment" 215), Moffett's integrated view of drama, speech, and writing would not emerge. If anything, such a distinction would only further obscure the very relations Moffett tries to uncover. For by its very nature purely analytical, categorical thought dissociates, producing typologies in theory and bureaucracies in practice. Categories and departments result from the same kind of thought.

And so, for Kinneavy drama is only a branch of literature, one of his four aims; for the educational establishment it is "theater arts," almost an extracurricular luxury, open to a few talented students and merely observed by the rest. But for Moffett, all the world's a stage; like Kenneth Burke, Moffett sees human experience as the interaction of persons, the "drama of human relations" (Rueckert xv). Instead of contrasting drama with other forms of discourse, Moffett views drama the way Burke does, as the hub of the whole universe of discourse (*Philosophy* 103), since drama *is* dialogue (conversation), soliloquy (thought, the internal conversation), and monologue (speech in the sense of public speaking). Drama even embraces writing in the sense that the ability to compose, to sustain written monologue, depends on the capacity to sustain oral monologue apart from the constant prompting and collaboration of others in conversation.

For Moffett, then, discourse is united in more than the grand abstraction *discourse*. Much more concretely, his universe of discourse is drama, and the other forms of discourse are consistent with drama because they arise from within the drama of human relations. And most especially, the various kinds of discourse are *not*, in Moffett's view, just so many isolated fragments of drama but are interconnected in such a way as to be ultimately indistinguishable. For Moffett, soliloquy is actually colloquy, the interaction of all the voices we internalize, voices that come to us first in dialogue; and soliloquy is what we select from and edit for both oral and written monologues. Moffett's discourse universe is seamless; his metaphor for it is "wheels within wheels" (48): Move one part of it, and all of it moves— like a complex clockwork.

A lovely concept, one might say, but what does it mean in practical, pedagogical terms? Moffett provided close to a full and detailed answer in the book he coauthored with Betty Wagner, *Student-Centered Language Arts and Reading, K-13*. The essentials are the following: First, one teaches discourse not by talking about it but by discourse activities coupled with constant feedback. Moffett's teacher is not a lecturer or a distant authority who assigns and grades but is someone who prestructures and guides the classroom, the arena in the drama of human relations. Second, since drama and speech are "base and essence" (*Teaching* 60), the development of writing ability should never be detached from the oral foundation of all language use. Writing should arise naturally out of oral interaction in the classroom, out of discussion and oral monologue. "Writing should be taught," Moffett claims, "as an extension of speech," because "much of writing technique is a matter of simulating or replacing vocal characteristics" (41). In the strongest possible terms he resists the dichotomizing of writing and speech that can easily result from a superficial reading of Walter Ong, who in the midst of exposing so well the chasm between oral and literature cultures repeatedly insists, in perfect agreement with Moffett, that all reading and writing have an oral base (*Presence* 18). Moffett, certainly recognizing the differences between speech and writing, still holds that the best way to teach writing is by constant juxtaposition and interaction with oral performance.

Third and finally, Moffett's understanding of the relation between orality and literacy works hand in hand with his developmental view of discourse as a whole to open the way to a better rationale for assignment sequencing. We have already seen how the abstractive scales (the I-you and I-it relations) help us to envision assignments that build on each other. Similarly, Moffett suggests progressions from the oral to the written, from, say, group discussion to soloing out of groups in oral monologue, to informal writing, to formal writing—all activities that might develop naturally from any serious exploration of a topic or problem. The key word here is *naturally*: What Moffett wants is an approach to teaching discourse as free as possible from artificial and arbitrary constraints. As we learn first to talk and then, laboriously, to write—as writing in the real world often is preceded by and precipitates much oral interaction—so our classrooms should move continuously from the oral to the written and back again. What arises from discussion should itself stimulate discussion rather than remain something simply to be graded. In sum, Moffett strives for a classroom as organic, as seamless, as his discourse theory itself.

Neglect of Purpose

Theories, like the people who construct them, are imperfect. It is hardly surprising, therefore, that the very moves that allowed Moffett his dynamic and integrated view of discourse are also responsible for the greatest single weakness in his theory, the lack of an explicit treatment of discourse purpose or function. When Moffett chose to emphasize *relations* among the elements in the triangle, the constructive potential of taking the elements of the triangle *in themselves* was lost; nothing comparable to Kinneavy's aims or Britton's functions could emerge.

In itself, of course, Moffett's neglect of purpose is only an omission, hardly a fault when one considers that no theory can be all-encompassing. Furthermore, some notion of purpose is certainly implicit in the I-you and I-it relations: If one insisted that Moffett's version of the communication triangle, "somebody-talking-to-someone-else-about-something," ought to have the additional phrase for-some-reason, he would surely assent. The problem here is not awareness but the systematic consequences, both theoretical and practical, of not having an explicit rationale of purpose. The following few sections deal with problems related directly and indirectly to the neglect of purpose.

A Digression on the Problem of Literature's Status

Even a cursory comparison of the general structure of Moffett's theory with Kinneavy's or Britton's will reveal that unlike Moffett, Kinneavy and Britton have a definite place for literature in their systems. Moffett is able to handle only those kinds of literature that incline toward narrative; lyric poetry, for example, he thinks cannot be located by the I-you and I-it relations. An awkward hiatus results within Moffett's conception of literature, a tacking on of poetry to his "spectrum of discourse" (see 47, and the discussion of the "mythic mode," 48–53).

For Kinneavy and Britton, who both view all literary genres as instances of an aim or a function of discourse, the problem Moffett wrestles with does not arise. Nor do Kinneavy and Britton run afoul of the confusion that afflicts Moffett when he tries to invoke Susanne Langer's distinction between discursive and presentational symbolism. For several reasons, however, we cannot simply reject Moffett and accept Kinneavy and Britton. We cannot assess any way of handling literature within a discourse theory at all until we decide whether literature is a form of discourse in the first place. Strangely enough, none of our theorists really addresses this question; they merely assume that literature must be included in any theory of discourse. However, given the modern history of the question from Kant on, such an unargued assumption cannot be made.

The case against taking literature as discourse is formidable. Aristotle sharply distinguished *poesis* from both rhetoric and dialectic; he classed *poesis* with other art forms, such as music, on the grounds that all are mimetic (McKeon 1455–57). His view is the distant source of all notions of literature as fine art: the poet uses words the way a painter uses color, texture, and form to construct an object of interest and beauty in itself. This view of literature makes it a concern of aesthetics rather than discourse theory.

No matter where one draws the conceptual lines, literature clearly differs from philosophical, scientific, and rhetorical discourse in the status of its assertions. "The poet," Sir Philip Sidney said, "never affirmeth" (294): whereas a philosopher or an orator makes statements about the world whose truth value and logical validity can be tested, only a very naive or deranged person would seek confirmation of the factual statements of Swift's persona in "A Modest Proposal." In short, we do not attach the credibility to literature that we do to a scientist's article or book: truth in literature is a matter of verisimilitude, compatibility with a fictive world; truth in science conforms to reality, the objective world external to consciousness. Using a like argument, Kant held that literature was a special case, exempt from the rigorous canons of truth he would apply to discourse proper (45–46).

Susanne Langer, whose thinking about literature parallels that of Aristotle and Kant in some respects, asserts that we tend to accept literature as discourse for no more elevated a reason than that literature looks like discourse, arranged on the page, for the most part, in sentences and paragraphs and seemingly making the same assertions. But for Langer, as for Kant, discourse uses the symbols of natural and artificial language to make assertions about reality, whereas a work of literature *is* a symbol, a self-contained fictive world, offering a "virtual image" of life, which because of its virtuality renders efforts at truth assessment irrelevant (*Feeling* 208, 369). And so Langer distinguishes as sharply between discursive and presentational symbols as Kant did between science and literature.

Do our theorists deal with literature as discourse simply because the field of English teaches so much literature? Perhaps the inclusion of literature within discourse is no more than a habit, a chance historical association with no solid intellectual grounding at all. Perhaps those who insist that the literature of an age should be taught in conjunction with its painting, sculpture, and music are on the right track, whereas those who equate literature's message with that of philosophy are just confusing art with discourse.

What can be said against the Aristotle-Kant-Langer contentions? We cannot simply ignore their argument by invoking long-established practice. A theory of discourse requires a theoretical justification for including literature within the universe of discourse. Kinneavy seems to offer this justification. The study of English or any other language amounts to a study of the language itself—its grammar in the extended linguistic sense of this term —and all uses of the language, its discourse, its pragmatics. Literature is certainly a use of the language and therefore a part of discourse. Implicit in Kinneavy's distinctions is a critique of the narrow notion of discourse typical of most philosophy. Preoccupied with the question of truth, philosophy tends to ignore or dismiss as trivial all uses of language other than the philosophical-scientific one. Mistaking their part for the whole, philosophers then set up sharp contrasts between discourse and literature. But many nonliterary uses of language, indisputably instances of discourse, cannot be assessed appropriately via the typical logical-empirical notion of truth. Expressive discourse, for example, cannot be so assessed: what can one say about the truth value of "We hold these truths to be self-evident, that all men are created equal . . ."? The point here is value articulation and not objective truth. Likewise, when we use language phatically, the question of truth is largely irrelevant. "Nice weather, isn't it?" though clearly an assertion, seldom occasions dialectical assessment. Where truth is not simply irrelevant it is often secondary: an orator seeks to persuade and fails as an orator insofar as persuasion is not achieved, no matter the truth value of what is said.

If literature is a special case, exempt from the Kantian critique, then so is most of the universe of discourse. If we attempt to exclude literature from discourse because it sometimes traffics in fictive worlds, we will have to exclude other instances of discourse on other counts. Faced with such unwieldy consequences, the Aristotle-Kant-Langer case against literature as a form of discourse collapses. Furthermore, taking literature as a form of discourse does not entail its rejection as a fine art. Both Kinneavy and Britton discuss literature in aesthetic terms. Indeed, literature is that aim or function of discourse for which aesthetic assessment is especially, but not exclusively, appropriate. Accepting literature as discourse, then, does not mean whole-sale denial of the Aristotle-Kant-Langer argument.

Moffett's Handling of Literature

Now that we can justify including literature in the universe of discourse, our question becomes exactly how to do it. Moffett both helps and hinders the finding of a satisfactory answer. On the one hand, his approach is conceptually unsound; on the other hand, Moffett excels all of our theorists in *integrating* literary discourse with other kinds of discourse.

Most of the time, Moffett provides the needed corrective to categorical thought; in this case, one must say that he only muddles categories. He invokes Langer's distinction between discursive and presentational symbols without apparently realizing that the distinction itself leads to excluding literature from discourse. Worse yet, he does not seem to grasp Langer's notion of presentational symbol. He considers it only in the context of poetry, whereas for Langer, all *poesis*, including drama and prose fiction, which Moffett places within his spectrum of discourse, amounts to presen-tational symbols. Hence the awkward hiatus noted before: Part of literature finds a definite place in Moffett's theory; another part is, without much justification, merely tacked on. Conceptually, then, Kinneavy's handling of literature is clearly better than Moffett's. Kinneavy does a better job with literature because he has a typology of aims; Moffett's neglect of purpose is at the root of his need to improvise with Langer's categories to justify treating poetry as a special case.

Paradoxically, Kinneavy gives us good reason to take literature as dis-course, but he then treats literature so formalistically, so much as an art object, that one could almost call him Kantian in this respect. The sense that literature "says" something about world or reveals world, and thus escapes the prison of self-containment, just does not emerge well in Kin-neavy. It does, however, in Moffett:

> The concrete aspect of story is misleading because . . . it actually compresses
> the logic of classes and the logic of propositions into a chronological mode.
> What psychoanalytical theories have called "condensation" in the primary-
> process thinking of dreams is, I feel sure, just this compression of three logics
> into one: concrete figures, objects, and settings are doubling as classes of
> experience; concrete actions as the relations among classes; and plots as syl-
> logisms. Hence so much rich ambiguity and potent symbolism. (52)

Clearly, Moffett not only says literature is discourse but treats literature as
discourse. His theory leads us to work with literature and other forms of
discourse together, allowing history to illuminate fictive history and vice
versa, encouraging, for example, a teacher to assign *A Journal of the Plague
Year* even as students are writing and getting responses to their own journals.
In this way we enrich the teaching of all discourse, creating the environment
for a thorough understanding of the differences between, say, a history and
a novel, as well as the *poesis* in all historical writing, the history in all *poesis*.

What we need to advance the theory of literature within a theory of
discourse is a synthesis of the best of Kinneavy with the best of Moffett.
Without realizing it, Britton partially accomplishes just such a synthesis, as
we shall see in the next chapter. It suffices to say at this point, however,
that Kinneavy brings his forte, conceptual clarity and systematic thought,
to our view of literary discourse, while Moffett brings his more concrete,
dynamic, relational view, cutting boldly across static, dissociative thought
about any kind of discourse.

Reduction of I-It to Information

One of the more convincing and insightful aspects of *Teaching the Universe
of Discourse* is Moffett's treatment of abstraction. He clarifies the concept
by showing us that abstraction is not only conceptual but also perceptual,
something that the naive empiricism of common sense constantly tends to
forget. Moffett not does merely discriminate kinds of abstraction; rather,
he relates them in a developmental hierarchy so that we see simultaneously
both the broad spectrum of intellectual activities that compose abstraction
and the functional relations among the kinds of abstraction. Furthermore,
he relates the ladder of abstraction to intellectual development generally and
especially to awareness of abstraction, itself an important dimension of
growth. All this is fundamental if we are to teach our students to play the
whole symbolic scale and to know where they are on it at any given time.

So brilliant is Moffett's handling of abstraction that it is easy to overlook
its limitations. Moffett points out that his theory is "based in the hierarchic
symbolizing of actualities, on information processing" (48). While most

discourse conveys at least some information, and granting that the transfer of information is a vital function of discourse and never absent from the total process of writing or reading, Moffett nevertheless leaves the impression that, excepting poetry's presentational symbolizing, all of discourse can be adequately grasped from the point of view of information processing. The obvious objection is that much of the universe of discourse, not just poetry, transmits information only secondarily, if at all. Performative discourse ("I pronounce you husband and wife") hardly tells its audience anything new. Most persuasive discourse seeks to structure or restructure what is well known to its audience. Likewise, exploratory discourse, whether as scientific theory or philosophical dialogue, seldom informs but instead seeks to explain the significance of what is known. In general, information processing offers a useful perspective for some discourse but cannot adequately handle the universe of discourse.

Moffett's reduction of I-it to information also prevents him from dealing directly with the kind of abstraction that goes on in, for example, persuasive discourse. The human ability to abstract operates not only in the supposedly disinterested spheres of science and history but also in what Kenneth Burke calls the "human barnyard," where selection from reality is not so much a matter of ascent up the dialectical ladder of abstraction as it is a function of "interest-begotten prejudice" (*Rhetoric* 23). But Moffett ignores this very important region in the universe of discourse almost altogether; the one kind of persuasive discourse he mentions, debate, is dismissed in favor of the gentler give and take of dialogue (96–97). It is as if Moffett desires to exclude the contentiousness of argumentation, the excitement of controversy, from the classroom, a bias that does not accord well at all with his dramatic pedagogy.

I cannot say why Moffett averts his attention from the human barnyard with its insistent, daily blandishments. But it requires no idle speculation to say that his apparent bias against persuasion will not help students play the whole symbolic scale. Quite the contrary, his focus on information processing serves to reinforce the tendency to assign only informative essays in school writing, a tendency that Britton strongly deplores (197–98). Furthermore, if Kinneavy is right in claiming that we encounter more persuasion—mostly in the form of advertising—than any other aim of discourse (212), we could well be failing to equip our students in a most crucial function of discourse.

At this point, we can begin to detect the truly serious consequences, both theoretical and practical, of Moffett's neglect of purpose. Undoubtedly these consequences help to explain why Britton, who follows Moffett in so many ways, departs from him in offering an explicit, systematic scheme of discourse functions.

Conclusion

I began my analysis of *Teaching the Universe of Discourse* by claiming that in some respects it is more advanced than Kinneavy's theory. In other respects, as in the difficulties stemming from the lack of systematic attention to purpose, it is less advanced. One might say, then, that Moffett provides a much-needed corrective to Kinneavy's static mode of thought while being at the same time in need of correction himself. Such is the dialectic implicit in our theories, pushing us on toward synthesis of the best of each.

But what about Moffett's achievement in itself? What accounts for the generally enthusiastic reception that *Teaching* had when it first appeared and the continuing interest it apparently still has since reissuance of the unrevised text? The key to its appeal is *integration*. "He has rare ability," the great psycholinguist Roger Brown wrote of Moffett, "to see relations among language study, the curriculum as a whole, and some of the general problems of our society" (xiii). We have seen how Moffett exposes the relations among kinds of discourse and how some kinds of discourse develop from others and lead to still other forms. But Moffett integrates far more than the universe of discourse; his view of that universe centers in drama and merges insensibly with his dramatic classroom, thoroughly integrating theory and praxis. And there is no question as to how his view of discourse accords with language and discourse development: the two are indistinguishable in Moffett's developmental theory of discourse, which always unites logic and psychologic in its curricular implications.

Moffett pulls together an extraordinary array of concerns normally dealt with in isolation from one another; this is precisely the source of his continuing appeal in a field still very far from knowing itself. He is able to do so because he is determined at the outset not to do what Kinneavy did in artificially isolating discourse to gain the scientific advantage of concentration by elimination. Moffett works with discourse in its living matrix and not as an isolatable concept apart from its context.

Part of this living matrix is thought, the philosophy always implicit in even the sketchiest of discourse theories. Philosophy, of course, is much more prominent in Kinneavy than in Moffett. Kinneavy derives his basic view of discourse from semiotics, from Charles Sanders Peirce via Charles Morris, and attempts to ground each aim of discourse in an appropriate philosophical context, for example, expressive discourse in early Jean-Paul Sartre (*Being and Nothingness*). But while philosophy is everywhere in *A Theory of Discourse*, the sense of an all-embracing viewpoint is obscured by Kinneavy's philosophical pluralism, laudable in itself but problematic in that Peirce is used for this, Sartre for that, Aristotle for still other ends, all in piecemeal fashion. In contrast, Moffett hints at *the* philosophy implicit in his view of discourse.

Like Martin Heidegger and Hans–Georg Gadamer, Moffett does not view language simply as something that people use as a tool. Rather, language is what we are; language is ontological, human-making (Gadamer, *Philosophical Hermeneutics* 3). Moffett cites G. H. Mead:

> I know of no other form of behavior than the linguistic in which the individual is an object to himself, and, so far as I can see, the individual is not a self in the reflective sense unless he is an object to himself. (66)

As Moffett explains, "self and mind are social artifacts, and the constituents of the self mirror the constituents of society; thought involves incorporating the roles and attitudes of others and addressing oneself internally as one would address another externally" (67). Language makes community possible and community is the source of self and thought, so that everything we are has a linguistic foundation.

Granted, there is nothing really new here: language-centeredness is almost what makes modern philosophy modern. One of "our own" has been telling us for half a century that human beings are symbol-using animals. No one but Moffett, however, has so explicitly integrated discourse theory with this dominant strain in modern thought.

To all his achievements we must add another, his attempts to locate discourse theory in the broader context of language-centered philosophy. This is not an interest one would expect to find in someone so concerned with the pragmatics of teaching English. Taken all in all, we could ask no more of our field's first contemporary discourse theorist.

CHAPTER THREE

BRITTON'S THEORY

Overview

As Kinneavy's theory centers in two concepts, aim and mode, and as Moffett's develops from two relations, I-you and I-it, so Britton's is also essentially confined to two terms, *function* and *audience*. Function in Britton seems to designate much the same thing as aim in Kinneavy. Both theorists use the term *expression* to refer to discourse focused on the writer's personal experience. Britton's category *poetic* corresponds to Kinneavy's literary aim; Britton's conative function is close to what Kinneavy means by persuasion; and both recognize an informative function or aim. The general impression is that the two typologies are hardly distinguishable.

In specifics, however, the two theorists diverge considerably. Unlike Kinneavy, Britton does not distinguish individual from group expression. Whereas Kinneavy holds that expression is only logically prior to other discourse aims, Britton attributes temporal priority to expression, citing Sapir's notion that speech, in the sense of everyday conversation, is predominantly expressive (10). Since children are first speakers of the language, it follows that expression is developmentally antecedent to the other functions.

The predominant expression of a child's talk and writing, however, is not the expressive discourse of adults. So Britton distinguishes immature from mature expression, advancing the former as a "kind of matrix from which differentiated forms of mature writing are developed" (83). Clearly nothing in Kinneavy's static model of discourse aims corresponds to Britton's positing of immature expression as the developmental matrix of all discourse. Indeed, only Britton among our theorists treats purpose developmentally.

Expression, then, really does not mean the same thing for Britton that it does for Kinneavy. Even their notions of mature expression diverge subtly. Britton, for example, stresses the *self-exploratory* motive in expression more than Kinneavy does; Kinneavy tends to see expression as an assertion of identity rather than a tentative or quizzical probing of identity. Likewise, when one turns to Britton's transactional functions, which correspond to Kinneavy's referential and persuasive aims, the sense of disparity mounts.

First, Kinneavy derives reference and persuasion from different points on the communication triangle—from reality (the objective or phenomenal world) and decoder (audience or reader) respectively—whereas Britton sees a single category, the transactional, subdivided into the informative and the conative. Second, Kinneavy distinguishes informative, exploratory, and scientific discourse within the referential aim. Though all three would presumably be types of transactional discourse in Britton's system, only the informative receives much attention; exploratory is mentioned under both expressive and transactional discourse; and scientific is not treated at all.

Third, Britton's term *conative* obviously does not mean the same thing as persuasion, since Britton subdivides the conative into regulative and persuasive discourse. Conative includes all "cases where an attempt to change one's behaviour, attitude, or opinion can be easily discerned" (94): Within this category, the regulative "gives instructions" and is "not concerned with giving information or putting forward reasons," since it functions mainly to control "actions and behaviours"; the persuasive, in contrast, centers more on the reader's "attitudes and opinions," attempting to influence them by "reason, argument, or strategy" (99). While Britton and Kinneavy essentially agree on the nature of persuasion, Kinneavy does not touch on the regulative at all.

We will shortly explore the implications of these differences; for now we need only note that much more than choice of terms sets Britton's treatment of the transactional functions apart from Kinneavy's referential and persuasive aims. Indeed, where the individual aims and functions are concerned, the two theorists come together in only two categories, the persuasive and what Britton calls the poetic function, Kinneavy the literary aim. What differences there are seem to me inconsequential; but with all the other functions or aims, the differences are in varying degrees significant and require us to make some difficult choices.

Britton's treatment of audience departs from both Kinneavy and Moffett. For Kinneavy, audience is implicit in aim to a large extent—given an informative aim, the audience becomes a gerundive, a "to be informed." For Britton, however, as for Moffett, audience is more an independent variable. And both Britton and Moffett treat audience awareness developmentally, a measure of writing maturity being the ability to adjust discourse to varying audiences, especially to the impersonal, public audience of most adult, printed discourse.

Where Moffett stresses the continuity between speech and writing, Britton stresses the discontinuity between them, especially as audience differs from reader. In language very similar to Walter Ong's in the now classic article "The Writer's Audience Is Always a Fiction," Britton contrasts the speaker's audience, which is present and to which the speaker can adjust in process, with the writer's reader, an imaginative construct of the writer. According to Britton, the writer must fictionalize, "represent to himself a context of situation" (61). Britton also points out, in complete agreement with Ong, that writers acquire the ability to fictionalize not so much from speech as from reading, by experience with the largely tacit norms of such written genres as the "business letter, official document, or short story" (62). The readers of literate discourse, then, are not simply for Britton an extension of the conversational interlocutor or of the monologuist's silent but present audience. Britton sees a qualitative difference here, while also agreeing with Moffett on the importance of the dialogic writing classroom in fostering a sense of the "other." Furthermore, Britton clearly recognizes the priority of speech not only in deriving his function categories from the undifferentiated expressiveness of conversation but also in his examples of early writing, which are no more than talk written down, showing virtually no discrimination between audience and reader.

Britton stresses growth *within* the writer's conception of reader, a notion only at best implicit in Moffett. For Moffett a student's ability to solo out of ensembles, to relinquish the supportive give-and-take of conversation and sustain oral monologues, is the pivotal act; Britton looks further down the developmental line to the perhaps more difficult transition from the teacher as reader (the internalized other) to the impersonal public as reader (the generalized other). Obviously, such a transition has everything to do with the difference between immature and mature writing, since the inferior-superior relation of student to teacher gives way to an adult relation of peers. And obviously this development is as late as Moffett's is early; many college students still are trying to second-guess their teachers rather than writing for some segment of the more abstract and hypothetical reading public.

In sum, *The Development of Writing Abilities (11–18)* offers a relatively well developed view of discourse functions, a view that both resembles and conflicts with Kinneavy's aims; it also develops the audience dimension well beyond both Kinneavy and Moffett, especially in being sensitive to the complex relations between orality and literacy. Britton explores as well variables in the writing process not mentioned by our other theorists. For instance, he reflects on the writer's attitude toward the task at hand, discriminating among involved, impelled, and perfunctory attitudes. Thus while Britton's theory is elaborated in only two dimensions, potentially it is multidimensional to a higher degree than either Kinneavy's or Moffett's. Consequently, his work in toto represents an appreciable advance over that of his two predecessors.

Analysis

We need to be mindful of certain facts about the Britton study at the outset. Most important, it is not a theory of discourse per se; it reports, rather, the results of a lengthy and intensive empirical study of student writing in England and draws inferences for teaching and research based on these results. As such, only part of *Development* is directly relevant here, mainly chapters 2, 4, 5, and 6, wherein the theory the Britton team used to make sense out of their database is articulated.

The theoretical dimension, however, cannot be ultimately separated from the empirical and pedagogical dimensions. The theoretical dimension is especially problematical because Britton did not take a theory and apply it to student scripts; rather, he developed his theory in part from experience with the scripts and in part from other sources (e.g., Jakobson; see Britton 13–14) as a way of accounting for the scripts. We have, then, a fairly typical instance of scientific exploration, a hypothetical thought construct compounded of inferences from experience with the phenomena under study and an integration of plausible models from past thought.

What is problematical is not so much the methodology as how to receive Britton's theory itself. On the one hand, it alone of our four theories is backed by more than the informal empiricism underlying the theory of any experienced writing teacher; presumably, then, it should have a special authority. On the other hand, the theory is clearly limited by the job it was designed to do. The fact, for instance, that a very high percentage of the student scripts were informative led Britton to a hyperdevelopment of this function relative to the others. The result is an unbalanced theory—understandably, justifiably, given his purpose—but unbalanced nevertheless. Furthermore, some of his function and audience categories probably have no equivalent outside the school context and therefore have little or no value for a general theory of discourse. Again, this is not a fault but only a limitation arising from what the theory was meant to do.

No doubt readers familiar with the details of Britton's theory could surmise from my overview that I have chosen to omit those parts of it not relevant to a general theory of discourse. I offer no comment about the empirical approach to discourse study in general, or about the design of

Britton's study in particular, or about the validity of the results and the worth of the implications drawn from them—all of which fall outside both my competence and the focus of this study. Finally, I allot no privileged position to Britton's theory on account of its empirical grounding. A theory dmust score points by advancing better ideas—more precise, more inclusive, subject to less refutation than those of competitors. We shall find ample reason to accord Britton's theory a special authority based on theoretical grounds of assessment alone.

Placing Britton's Theory

Having developed Kinneavy and Moffett as thesis and antithesis respectively, I would now seem committed to Britton as a synthesis, as a Hegelian *aufgehoben*, a theory that simultaneously transcends, cancels, and preserves the opposing viewpoints toward discourse represented by Kinneavy and Moffett. While such is indeed my view I would not purchase symmetry at the price of inaccuracy. In some respects, seen in the context of his two predecessors Britton is synthetic; in other respects he is antithetical, countering Kinneavy or Moffett; and in still others he is neither, just different from or other than. I am striving, then, to achieve both a pattern and a complex picture.

Consider, for instance, Britton's treatment of discourse function: it preserves Kinneavy's emphasis on purpose as a prime variable, significant in that apparently neither theorist was aware of the other's work and because Britton asserts the centrality of function independently of Moffett (who otherwise influenced him significantly and whose neglect of purpose we noted in the last chapter). Britton's notion of function also transcends Kinneavy in offering both a view of mature discourse types and the beginnings of a dynamic or developmental view of discourse types (which is absent from Kinneavy's theory). Britton's continuum of functions, furthermore, may be said to cancel Kinneavy's tendency toward the flat choice in the classification of actual discourses. Like Kinneavy, Britton holds that most discourse is multifunctional, tending in any particular case more or less toward the dominance of one function over the others; but this "more or less" is better represented by Britton's continuum of functions than by Kinneavy's desire to force the issue, to see whenever possible one dominant aim and a subordinate relationship for any others. While, of course, Kinneavy's foreground-background conception may usually be adequate, theoretically we must side with Britton because distinguishable kinds of anything seem clearly demarcated only on account of conceptual idealization, while experience offers more shadings and gradations than sharp divisions.

Finally, Britton's functions are simply different from Kinneavy's aims in several respects. For one, Britton develops his continuum of functions in relation to a continuum of roles (i.e., participant-spectator); no such role continuum exists in Kinneavy.

If in general, then, Britton's theory can be viewed as an unintended synthesis of Kinneavy and Moffett, it is so only in part and imperfectly. It is also only in part and imperfectly an advance on Kinneavy and Moffett, for we shall discover good reasons to prefer various formulations of Kinneavy and Moffett over Britton.

The Concept of Function

Britton's notion of discourse function synthesizes Kinneavy and Moffett, the static or structural view with the dynamic or developmental view. What Britton does in essence is combine Kinneavy's focus on ideal, adult discourse competence with Moffett's focus on steps toward that competence. In his own words, "We must base our model on mature adult competence, if we are to trace stages in development towards that competence" (5). And so Britton's mature functions correspond to Kinneavy's aims, while his notion of immature expression as matrix and the hypothesis that part of growth is the increasing ability to discriminate the various functions and to perform focally in one of them answer more to Moffett's approach.

Britton's treatment of function poses a number of questions for this study, questions preliminary to any effort to synthesize our four theories. Since only Britton and Kinneavy have well-developed theories of discourse purpose, the questions center on the subtle tensions that underlie their apparent similarity. We might as well begin with the question, Should we prefer Kinneavy's term aim or Britton's term function? since logically this general question takes precedence over specific questions about the individual functions or aims.

Conceptually, function and aim have very different implications. As noted in the Kinneavy chapter, aim strongly suggests a subject, someone to take aim, and an object, something aimed at. One cannot ponder aim for long without thinking intent. Function, however, has no such implications. A hammer is designed for driving nails or tacks, but it may function as a paperweight or a lethal weapon. Similarly, I might write a memo, the intent of which is to inform my colleagues of a meeting, but for those insiders who already know the subject, place, and time of the meeting, the memo functions as a formal announcement and not as information. Given these differences in implication alone, we can see that the choice between aim and function is no indifferent matter. Aim leads to intent (even if Kinneavy repressed this implication of his own term to avoid the intentional fallacy);

function does not commit us to intent so clearly or directly though the design of something does restrict its functioning.

If we must decide between aim and function, on what grounds should our decision be made? One could argue that aim and function cover different aspects of our complex intuitions about purpose. However difficult they may be to characterize, we do have intentions; and we have all experienced the difference between what we meant a discourse to do and what it actually did. Perhaps, then, our best move is to delimit the two notions carefully and use them more self-consciously, the yield being a more precise vocabulary for discussing purpose. Such a move, however, only dodges the issue at hand. Our task is not to develop an adequate philosophical view of purpose but to advance that notion of purpose best serving the typological needs of a theory of discourse. From this perspective, aim is better than function. A discourse's function is always relative to historical conditions and is therefore forever indeterminate; a discourse's function depends on who uses it. The Gospels, as the name implies, were originally testimonies of faith meant to win or strengthen adherence, but they have functioned for the unsophisticated as history, as purely and simply an account of what happened. In contrast, modern scholars find another use for the same accounts: not history per se but a source for histories. And so on: function depends on a reader's interests and purposes and therefore is too unstable a concept for discourse classification.

We must, then, opt for aim over function. The aim concept, however, poses problems of its own. I have already given reasons to reject Kinneavy's objective, formalistic treatment of aim, which holds that aim inheres in a discourse itself. Aim is always a judgment, an interpretation—of my own motives as I am writing, of what the situation calls for or the audience expects or needs, or of the motives of another writer—really an inference based on the discourse and what I happen to know about its situational context. Discourses have aims only in the sense that someone designed them to achieve some end and that human beings respond to them as purposeful constructs. Otherwise they are just sounds or marks on a page.

If not in the discourse itself, then, where do aims reside? The answer must be in *convention*—intersubjective "agreement" (mostly tacit knowledge; see Polanyi 69–245) about the norms of a discourse type. The efforts of Britton and Kinneavy to describe the aims must then be understood as an explicit formulation of our tacit knowledge about typical features of discourse of a certain type.

Such an intersubjective understanding of aim overcomes the liabilities of Kinneavy's formalism—we need not, for example, attribute aim to inanimate texts—but does it provide a more stable concept for discourse classification than function does? My answer is Yes, but only relatively. Whereas function depends heavily on *my* attitudes, needs, knowledge, expectations, and so on, aim depends on a more collective awareness of "what counts as what." Convention changes, of course, so that, for example, ancient oratory and oratorical theory exemplify and isolate for discussion some features no longer typical of persuasive speaking; but convention at least changes slowly, slowly enough to permit discourse classification. Furthermore, convention by its very nature excludes the more idiosyncratic dimensions of function.

Understood as a judgment about the purpose(s) of a discourse or of a partial discourse in the making, aim offers relative stability and thus lends itself to the typological needs of discourse theory. Taking aim as a judgment or an interpretation based on convention has many other advantages as well. We need not repress or suppress any of the implications of the term *aim* itself, for clearly the objective target is discourse of a recognizable type, while the subjective dimension of aim includes sharing with the audience tacit knowledge of discourse norms. Furthermore, identifying aim with convention is consonant with Britton's emphasis on convention and his hypothesis that part of a writer's development is increasing ability to differentiate discourse types and therefore to sustain performance in accord with the norms of a dominant aim. Such development is necessarily slow and imperfect, since tacit knowledge of anything is an unconscious process of internalization based on experience, on "knowing how" rather than on "knowing that." Finally, the notion of aim as convention supports both Moffett's dramatic classroom and the traditional view of rhetoric as a conscious art. Tacit knowledge of discourse conventions depends on immersion, on much reading and writing across the spectrum of discourse types—exactly what Moffett's pedagogy would achieve. The young student especially needs to discourse, not hear about discourse. The art of rhetoric amounts to conscious formulation of tacit knowledge and therefore depends utterly on tacit knowledge as its foundation (since we can never completely articulate the "knowing how" of something so complex as discourse). Nevertheless, the art of rhetoric is invaluable, superior to immersion alone, because conscious knowledge of convention is far more likely to result in reliable selection of means. When the student is ready (roughly at the onset of formal operations), Moffett's dramatic classroom must be supplemented by gradual exposure to the rhetoric of all the mature aims of discourse.

But what exactly are the mature aims of discourse? We have now a hypothetical concept of purpose suitable for developing a discourse typology, but we still have the problem of competing typologies, Britton's divisions in the universe of discourse versus Kinneavy's. And so in the next few sections we turn to the individual aims or functions themselves and to the question of whose list merits theoretical endorsement.

Britton's Three Main Function Categories

A significant difference between Kinneavy's aim model and Britton's function model is the absence in Kinneavy of any sharp dichotomy or opposition of discourse types. Kinneavy's aims amount to four distinct types of equal value; the model itself does not suggest that expression is the opposite of persuasion, or persuasion the opposite of science, or anything the opposite of anything else. We have just an array of purposes, the conventions of each aim *contrasting* to varying degrees with the others. But no two aims are conceived as polar opposites.

The very logic of Britton's model, however, requires polar opposition. For he conceives the functions as a line continuum, and one cannot have such a continuum without the extremes to define end points for the continuum. Thus the logic of Britton's model encourages sharp contrast of transactional functions with the poetic. In fact, Britton offers a list of flatly opposed features under the heading "Contrasting the extremes: transactional and poetic" (93–94). Although we might see the polarization of these two functions as a convenience, a deliberate oversimplification to aid the assessors in allocating scripts, still one must recognize a tendency toward dichotomy in the very structure of Britton's model.

We can detect this tendency in Britton's opening move. He does not begin, as Kinneavy does, with the communication triangle; instead he contrasts two roles, participant versus spectator. "Given that man constructs a representation of the world as he has experienced it *in order to operate in it*," Britton says, "an alternative kind of behavior is then open to him: he may manipulate the representation *without seeking outcomes in the actual world*" (79–80). Britton's next move is to associate these roles with two functional extremes: the writer as participant is using language "to get things done," as a transaction to "inform, advise, persuade, instruct" (88); the writer as spectator is using language poetically, "as an art medium," to make "a verbal construct, an 'object' made out of language" (90), whose function is to "please and satisfy the writer" and the reader. That is, "poetic writing constitutes language that exists *for its own sake* and not as a means of achieving something else" (91).

Had Britton developed merely a distinction between the transactional and the poetic, I would object only to the formalistic language used to characterize the poetic function, as I have before in discussing Kinneavy. But Britton does not just distinguish—he dichotomizes, treating the transactional and the poetic as polar opposites. Such a relation idealizes in the bad sense of misrepresenting reality. On the one hand, one does not have to search hard for literature that wants to get things done ("justify the ways of God to man"); on the other hand, one often reacts aesthetically to a metaphor or a turn of phrase or a graphic in a persuasive or informative discourse. These facts do not defeat a distinction; they do, however, indicate the excessive idealization of a dichotomy between the transactional and the poetic.

The exact problem here is not a defect of insight. Like Kinneavy, Britton stresses that purpose is seldom single, seldom pure, that actual discourses tend only toward a dominant purpose. Furthermore, he notes at one point that his team of researchers experimented with such categories as poetic-conative and poetic-expressive. The problem instead is his model, which fails to depict his own insights adequately. Rather than a single continuum that opposes the transactional and the poetic, we need Kinneavy's array of purposes and continua between all the aims or functions. While such a conception may strain the resources of graphic representation, it is better to forgo graphics altogether, if necessary, than to essentialize one's view of discourse in a model that suggests false dichotomies.

Mature Expression in Britton

What I am proposing is that we retain Kinneavy's basic model of the mature aims—deriving them as he does from the communication triangle—while incorporating into his model Britton's valuable notion of continuum, using it to recognize gradations between the aims. In doing so we can achieve Susanne Langer's theoretical ideal of concepts with "definite centers and labile limits" (*Mind* 260), highly desirable in that we cannot think without concepts with specifiable content and cannot apply our concepts sensitively without recognizing many instances that fall clearly neither here nor there. We also avoid relationships between the aims of mere opposition, which tends only to reinforce oversimplification. Thus when Britton contrasts the extremes of his continuum, he not only loses the "labile limits" of his concepts but also lends support to the pernicious split between so-called creative writing and all other kinds of writing.

So far as Britton's three main discourse functions are concerned, adopting Kinneavy's model leaves us with one final problem—what to do with expressive discourse. Britton's model places expressive discourse in the middle of his continuum between the transactional and the poetic, as if to indicate its centrality among the mature functions. This impression of centrality is reinforced by his view of the other two functions as movements away from expressive discourse. Mature expression, then, for Britton has something of both the transactional and the poetic, of both the participant and the spectator. However, "the demands of a *task*, the need to *do* something by means of language, will, if taken far enough, change the expressive into the transactional . . . ; the demands of the *construct*, the urge to *make* something in language and the intricacies of doing so, will, if taken far enough, change the expressive into the poetic" (93). Both movements, Britton notes, are "from an intimate to a more public audience" (83).

In contrast, expressive discourse in Kinneavy's model is just one among four major aims, none of them being central or pivotal with respect to the others. Adopting Kinneavy's model, then, entails rejecting the central position of Britton's expressive discourse. And there are good reasons to dispute any privileging of expressive discourse so far as our model of mature aims is concerned. I have no grounds for questioning the developmental priority of immature expression; quite the contrary, my own intuitions about the discourse of young children match Britton's—that it is largely undifferentiated by function and in the main expressive. Given the egocentricity of children, given their lack of experience with literacy in general and with the conventions of adult discourse in particular, and given the intimate audience of the family, I do not see how their discourse could be other than as Britton describes it. Expressive discourse, then, is central in the sense that it is the trunk from which the various branches of the mature aims grow.

Expressive discourse, however, has no special claim in a theory of adult discourse aims. Here we must not confuse the *expressive impulse* (itself discursive) with *expressive discourse*. Apart from the imposed task, all language use arises from the need to have one's say—from the expressive impulse. In children, to the delight and dole of their parents, the expressive impulse issues in expressive discourse, in saying what they happen to think or want regardless of appropriateness. Part of adult-level competence is the ability to gauge a discourse situation and to function within the conventions appropriate to the situation. The expressive impulse in adults may result in discourse in any of the mature aims, with no special inclination toward expressive discourse per se.

Furthermore, contrary to Britton's identification of expression with an intimate audience, much mature expression is quite public. Manifestos, for instance, are clearly directed to the world at large, as are declarations, and essays of the what-I-believe sort. For adults an expressive discourse can be just as public as the discourse Britton identifies with the transactional or the poetic, and just as much a means of doing something as anything Britton would class as transactional.

If the expressive impulse in children spontaneously takes the form of immature expression, then it seems reasonable to hold, as Britton does, that mature expression ought to be the adult function most congenial to a child's interests and experience. If children can most readily function in mature expression first, clearly they must gradually learn to suppress or edit out those aspects of expression that interfere with transactional or poetic discourse. In this sense, one may speak of movements away from expressive discourse. But a model of ideal, adult-level competence ought not to imply, as Britton's does, that any of the aims or functions are more central, pivotal, or basic than the others. Nor should it restrict the concept of mature expression to individual self-expression for an intimate audience. Since Kinneavy's model and concept does neither of these, his treatment of expression is preferable to Britton's.

The Transactional Category

Turning now from the issue of the basic model for adult-level competence, we must confront next the questions raised by the differing categories and subcategories of the mature aims or functions. At the highest level of division, Britton posits the transactional function and subdivides it into the informative and the conative, whereas Kinneavy discriminates two aims, the referential and the persuasive, subdividing referential into the informative, the exploratory, and the scientific. The first question, then, is whether we should postulate one large category, the transactional, from which we derive all uses of the language to get things done—to, for example, inform, persuade, and instruct—or should we dissociate informing from persuading by deriving them as Kinneavy does from different points on the triangle.

In a sense, this question has been settled if not answered. For if my arguments against Britton's one-dimensional continuum of functions are accepted, we are left with Kinneavy's aim model as the only other purpose-based typology offered by our four theorists. However, the question ought to be addressed independently of what our previous conclusions may imply.

Independent assessment is especially important, for there are significant problems with Britton's transactional concept and Kinneavy's rationale for splitting reference from persuasion. And neither is fully satisfactory. The transactional concept has a certain commonsense appeal: how a poem or a novel engages us differs qualitatively from a memo or a scientific article, whether we are writers or readers. But the definition "language to get things done" irresistibly suggests that there is some kind of language that does not get things done. And this is false. For even if one holds with W. H. Auden that poetry is not efficacious but just "survives in the valley of its making" (370), it is still a making, an act. Furthermore, it gets things done for both the poet and his reader. Denying this premise means denying Heidegger's view of all art as a mode of revelation, Kenneth Burke's treatment of literature as symbolic action, and virtually all theories of *poesis* prior to the Romantic movement.

The rejoinder, of course, is that poetry does not get things done in the same sense that, say, a technical report or a lawyer's brief does. And to that one must agree. We must distinguish ways of getting things done with language rather than postulating language that gets things done versus language that doesn't. And this means rejecting Britton's transactional concept, since its commonsense foundation collapses under careful scrutiny.

Kinneavy's distinction between reference and persuasion is rooted also in common sense. The very notion of referential discourse, for example, depends on two problematic assumptions: that there is reality in the sense of a material, objective world that exists apart from anyone's perceptions of it and that language can somehow refer to reality so conceived. Both assumptions are in serious and probably permanent dispute, but people act as if both assumptions were true. The very notion of persuasive discourse implies belief in the ability of a language act to change minds and behavior, and even the behaviorist, who would refuse to postulate mind, acts as if there were minds that can be changed when he argues for his theoretical position. Kinneavy does not really address, much less resolve, the philosophical issues implicit in the referential and persuasive categories. He assumes realism, referentiality, human choice, and a good deal more, including the key distinction between reference and persuasion, or truth versus opinion—that which is true versus that which is true for someone.

Kinneavy says that reference discourse foregrounds reality. What does this statement mean? It means, first, realism, a world external to mind, and second, language that can function to represent or characterize that world. From realism and referentiality, then, comes truth in its usual conception —correspondence—a match between what is and what is said about what is. So the notion of foregrounding reality entails the notion of objective truth—that which is true regardless of whether or not everyone subscribes to it. Each of Kinneavy's three divisions of reference discourse depend on truth as correspondence: One cannot speak of deliberate misinformation or inadvertent misrepresentation in informative discourse without truth as correspondence, and clearly it makes no sense to be in search of truth (exploratory discourse) or to advance demonstrations of hypotheses taken as establishing truth (scientific discourse) apart from the same standard.

It follows, therefore, that when Kinneavy distinguishes reference discourse from persuasion by saying that the former foregrounds reality while the latter foregrounds the decoder, he also implies that persuasion focuses on that which is true for someone: the persuader succeeds not simply by virtue of saying that which is so but only insofar as the audience assents to the saying. By convention (and the aims, we have said, do nothing more than make explicit the tacit norms of discourse kinds), reference discourse is charged with the objective dimension of truth, while persuasion is charged with the subjective dimension of truth.

I have developed the implications of Kinneavy's categories at some length for one reason primarily, to show what we are buying into should we accept provisionally his reference-persuasion distinction rather than Britton's transactional category. I have offered reasons to discard the latter, which leaves us, so far as our four theories are concerned, with the reference-persuasion distinction. For those unable to accept the notion of objective truth as opposed to truth for someone—and I cannot, as my commentary on Kinneavy's treatment of scientific discourse confirms—what we need to recognize is that the issue in question is a matter of convention, not our personal philosophies. We need not accept that reference discourse ever achieves any more than an approximation to its own standards, a more or less reliable or serviceable construction (interpretation) of reality that we may accept provisionally until new data or a better (more adequate or more functional) interpretation is advanced. We need only grant that reference discourse in Western culture conventionally shoots for truth as correspondence and is typically assessed by criteria derived directly or indirectly from the same standard. (Here the notion of aim is especially felicitous.)

Furthermore, we need not demote persuasion on the grounds of its concern with subjective truth. Very often the truths of persuasion (e.g., that democracy is preferable to tyranny) have more to do with our daily lives than any "truth" advanced by scientific discourse. And we can also point out that scientific paradigms must, too, be argued for, that without persuasion the intersubjective consensus upon which normal science depends cannot be achieved. Discovering "the truth" about anything is no triumph if we cannot induce others to believe it.

Whatever theoretical problems we have with the reference-persuasion distinction, there may be good reason to celebrate its practical impact. In his examination of student scripts, Britton observes that a very high percentage were informative. On the theoretical level, the best way to counter the typical schoolroom obsession with informative writing is not to derive information and persuasion from the same "higher" category, as Britton does, but rather to set them apart, as Kinneavy does, at the first level of division; it will be here that the persuasive aim will find greater presence.

Summation: Further Comments on Aims and Functions

We have yet to consider certain comparatively minor differences between Britton's model and Kinneavy's, the most important being the conative function versus the persuasive aim. Before taking these matters up, however, it may help to review where we are with respect to the general problem of a discourse typology.

Those drawn to Britton's model may feel that I have allowed Kinneavy's model a triumphant march over Britton's. I would insist, however, that if anything has emerged triumphant it is the dialectical give-and-take between the theories. I cite in evidence the following considerations. If I have argued for Kinneavy's typology over Britton's, I have done so only at the level of ideal, adult competence. The developmental dimension belongs wholly to Britton, whose basic view seems sound. I believe that immature expression is the developmental matrix of all discourse; that in teaching discourse we should develop the expressive function first as a kind of touchstone (the other functions being in this sense movements away from expression and toward the norms of the other functions); and that development in the dimension of the functions increases a student's ability to discriminate reliably among them and perform focally within them.

All of this I accept in the provisional, theoretical sense of acceptance—until a body of research or experience should accumulate to confirm, disconfirm, or force revision. What I have rejected in Britton I have actually accepted with modification. Thus, I have argued that the single, line continuum of discourse functions is simplistic and misleading; that it suggests a divorce between practical discourse and literature; and that it implies a centrality for expressive discourse that, apart from informal conversation, it probably does not have in the world of adult discourse, especially adult writing. However, I have argued for the notion of a continuum itself, for a distinction, but not a dichotomy, between poetic and other uses of language, and for the centrality of the expressive impulse in the sense that all discourse not simply imposed as a task begins as the desire to say something.

In short, what I have found reason to reject in Britton I have largely revised into acceptance; conversely, what I have accepted from Kinneavy I could only accept by rejecting, or revising, much of his thought. For example, so far as the needs of a discourse typology are concerned, I have advocated the concept of aim over function. But the specific concept I have advanced is not Kinneavy's view that aim inheres, objectively, in a text but rather that aim designates the conventions of a discourse type held intersubjectively by a language community, a culture. And if I have preferred Kinneavy's basic model of the aims over Britton's model of the functions, I have not simply endorsed Kinneavy's view of the individual aims themselves, several of which seem seriously flawed. To approach an adequate discourse theory one must compensate somehow for Kinneavy's omissions—the lack, for example, of a developmental view of the aims, of a theory of the composing process, of an understanding of audience/reader as a variable partly independent of purpose. One can find all of these in Britton.

Thus, no single theorist has been allowed a triumphant march. Even Moffett, who, because of his lack of a discourse typology based on purpose, has not played a role in this discussion, has at least one contribution to make, namely to the poetic or literary aim. As noted before, both Britton and Kinneavy would take literature as discourse, but both perceive it in terms that lead to its inclusion among the fine arts rather than as a type of discourse. Only Moffett treats literature *as discourse*, as a mode of indirect statement, as symbolic action in the world; only his view of literature justifies including it in a theory of discourse.

It is the dialectical give-and-take, then, the spirit of permanent revisionism, that governs my efforts, not a dogmatic preference for one theorist over another.

We have still some choices to make about the details of our aim model. For instance, shall we adopt Kinneavy's term *persuasive* for the audience-centered aim or Britton's term *conative*, which he subdivides into the regulative and the persuasive? Here Britton clearly has the comparative advantage. Kinneavy's scheme allots no place to a prominent type of discourse, the regulative, the giving of instructions or orders. Not only does Britton's model draw attention to this type of discourse that Kinneavy neglects, but he also correctly places the regulative: for, clearly, regulative discourse is audience- or reader-centered, but not persuasive in that typically no explicit appeals for assent are offered. Indeed, typical or central instances of regulative discourse differ from typical or central instances of persuasion precisely in the relation between encoder and decoder. Normally in regulative discourse the speaker or writer has an unquestioned authority, and compliance to some degree is simply taken for granted, whereas the persuasive speaker/writer cannot command but must convince, appealing explicitly through reason, emotion, and his or her own character for the assent of the auditor/reader.

Turning now from the conative aim to reference discourse, we encounter again in Britton's handling of exploratory writing a problem already discussed in the Kinneavy chapter: the placement of exploratory discourse. On the one hand, Britton sees exploratory discourse much as Kinneavy does, including it among the transactional functions, to "explain and explore ideas, construct theories"; on the other hand, he includes in expression "thinking aloud on paper," writing "intended for the writer's own use" (88). Apparently, then, Britton discriminates two kinds of exploration, one expressive and private, the other transactional and public. That such a discrimination corresponds to recognizably different kinds of discourse seems self-evident. The public business of theory construction, scientific or otherwise, is clearly not much like thinking aloud on paper or keeping a notebook or journal of one's own thoughts or responses to the thoughts of others. Britton's distinction should admonish us that exploratory discourse takes an array of forms, including one-on-one discussion, public forums, theory articulation, critiques of theories, the attempt to, as it were, write oneself out of an intellectual quandary or moral dilemma, and so on. Exploratory discourse in general, then, is not what Kinneavy tends to make it: public, scientific theory making. While, obviously, this dimension of exploration is quite salient and significant, it cannot be equated with exploratory discourse as a whole.

Britton's discrimination, then, opens up our notion of exploration, especially in his recognition that one way in which kinds of exploration differ from one another is along the private-public dimension. However, I think we gain nothing by obscuring the distinction between expressive and exploratory discourse. Thinking aloud on paper may have as its focus an effort to articulate the beliefs, attitudes, feelings, and experiences of the writer as individual or as spokesperson, but there is no necessary connection between such writing and expressive discourse. On the contrary, in my own experience at least, most such writing has nothing directly to do with individual or group identity but centers on a particularly thorny business, technical, or administrative problem, an intellectual or moral dilemma, a key professional decision, or the like. Now, of course, thinking aloud on paper involves, as any writing does, the character of the writer's life world. The point is that it need not and usually does not qualify as 'encoder-centered' or expressive discourse. The same can be said for "writing intended for the writer's own use." Such writing may be expressive, as in some diaries and journals, but it may just as well take the form of a scholar's notebook or even a list of tasks for the day.

In short, Britton broadens the view of exploration one finds in Kinneavy, who wants to link scientific theorizing (one form of exploratory discourse) with scientific discourse proper (with demonstration, efforts to confirm or disconfirm a hypothesis). As such, Britton's view of exploration is salutary. However, he is just wrong to identify thinking aloud on paper with expressive discourse. Probably the majority of such writing is private exploration, amounting to an externalization (because it is written down) of an internal dialectic, a debate with oneself. Even where the focus is the highly personal world of the writer, we can and ought to discriminate between a discourse that asserts that world and a discourse that examines the assertions. The former would be expressive discourse, a kind of didacticism aimed at the self, the latter, exploratory discourse, a dialectic of the self with the self. Where the two appear together, the judgment of aim is what it nearly always is in any instance—a question of relative proportion.

So far as our aim model is concerned, the above discussion proposes that we not include Britton's "thinking aloud on paper" or "writing intended for the writer's own use" as part of our description or understanding of expressive discourse. We are not thereby prevented, however, from taking some instances of both as expressive discourse when they in fact truly center on the encoder. The above discussion also proposes that we follow Britton in taking a wider view of exploration than Kinneavy's concentration on scientific theory suggests. Minimally we will have to distinguish between private and public exploration, though there can be no theoretical reason for stopping with only these two. Distinguishing between oral and written, for example, may be especially useful with respect to exploratory discourse.

Such thoughts lead to a general question implicit in Britton's seven sub-categories of the informative function: Where ought we to stop in dividing and subdividing within our major aims or functions? That is, how fine-grained should our typology be? This question has, of course, no theoretical answer. How much is enough is a matter of *practical need*. Britton elaborated on Moffett's I-it categories to produce his seven categories of informative discourse, not because he was compelled to do so out of theoretical considerations but because so high a percentage of the student scripts were informative. To do anything meaningful with them, he had to make distinctions. In a like manner we might elaborate any of the aims for some practical end—e.g., for an advanced composition course that centers on persuasion and therefore requires relatively detailed distinctions within that aim. Providing that the categories work, serving the practical need at hand, I cannot see any grounds for objections; at the same time, we ought not to confuse categories arising from practical need with categories demanded by a theoretical structure or by concrete reflection on discourse itself.

Only the latter two have standing so far as a general theory of discourse is concerned. As teachers of discourse, we will make whatever discriminations we need to help our students write and speak better; as theorists of discourse, we can admit only those discriminations that arise from a systematic view of discourse or from inadequacies detected in a systematic view through efforts to apply it to actual discourses. Although theory making always involves a dialectical interaction between guiding concepts and concrete reflection on the subject matter the concepts would characterize, so that the difference between system and application is often difficult to detect, we can see the difference more or less clearly, for example, in Kinneavy. His four discourse aims are justified by a theoretical construct; given the communication triangle and the concept of foregrounding, they follow almost with the logical rigor of a syllogism's conclusion. Thus, the category reference discourse is a good example of what I mean by a distinction demanded by a theoretical structure. However, his referential subcategories —the informative, exploratory, and scientific—are not deduced from the triangle but arise presumably from concrete reflection on discourse itself, including, especially in Kinneavy, the history of discourse types. Similarly, my reasons for preferring Britton's conative category to Kinneavy's persuasive category arose, not from considerations of the aim model itself, but from the recognition that there is a significant kind of adult discourse, the regulative, which is audience-centered but not persuasive.

There are, so to speak, rules of the game for developing the typology advanced here. For the purposes of this study, I shall be content if the aim concept and typology offered in this chapter are adjudged better than Kinneavy alone or Britton alone. For all I have promised is a synthesis of theories that will take us beyond where we would be if our guiding concepts were pure Kinneavy or pure Britton. At the same time, any theorist must be interested in the general question of how to develop or question any typology with a theoretical claim. Development is largely a matter of testing a provisionally accepted model against the subject matter it would comprehend, the object being to refine or elaborate without doing fundamental damage to the theoretical construct itself. While the motive to develop may have its origin in praxis, considerations of system alone distinguish theoretical development from the usually ad hoc nature of categories worked out for practical needs. Radical questioning, in contrast, takes on a double burden: it must show, on the one hand, that an existing model is inherently flawed; on the other, it must advance a model that overcomes the inadequacies of the existing model without producing undesirable consequences of its own. I have tried to show that Britton's function concept and functional model are inherently inadequate for purposes of a discourse typology and that Kinneavy's aim concept and model, suitably modified, avoids the problems that beset Britton without involving us in insuperable difficulties of its own making. If no such difficulties are discovered, then the task remaining is one of development, the never-ending process of securing the fit between how things are and how we say things are.

Conclusion

The principal impediment to synthesizing a single, coherent theory out of the best of our four theories is the conflict posed by Britton's functions and Kinneavy's aims: hence, the amount of attention devoted in this chapter to the questions connected with the aim concept and model. But Britton's theory is hardly confined to this functional dimension or variable. Certain other contributions require noting, both in themselves and in relation to Moffett and Kinneavy.

As discussed in the overview to this chapter, Britton chooses to develop extensively one other variable besides function in his potentially multidimensional theory, that of audience/reader. He offers, in fact, an extensive

audience typology used in assessing the student scripts that may have a
more general significance for further empirical research into the sense of
audience developed by student writers. We must attend, however, to Britton's audience concept itself, rather than to how it is used in his study, and
attend to it in relation to Moffett and Kinneavy and the needs of a general
theory of discourse.

"The sense of audience," according to Britton's definition, "is revealed
by the manner in which the *writer* expresses a *relationship* with the *reader* in
respect to his (the writer's) *undertaking*" (65–66). Britton endorses Moffett's
view that audience is not an abstract entity but a concrete relation between
writer and reader (Moffett's I-you), a relation of complementary roles. If
a writer casts himself or herself as an expert, the reader must necessarily be
less informed, at a lower level of understanding, so far as the particular
undertaking at hand is concerned. For Britton and Moffett, then, audience
cannot be approached in the way Kinneavy attempts to approach discourse
and aim, abstracting discourse from situation and aim from audience so that
he may consider "discourse in itself" and "aim in itself" in accord with
scientific habits of idealization. While this method of concentration by elimination has obvious advantages in general, the approach to audience by
abstraction, by drawing away from writer and undertaking, eliminates at
the outset the very relationships by which audience can be grasped. Given
the basic moves he makes, Kinneavy has little choice but to do what he
does—derive audience from aim, which is consistent with his elevation of
aim to the variable of variables but not very helpful in explaining how
discourse within the same aim may be conceived for different audiences.

In short, not only is the Britton-Moffett conception of audience preferable
to Kinneavy's because it has greater explanatory power, but their approach
is preferable also because audience cannot be handled by way of abstract
isolation from other relevant discourse variables. Furthermore, whereas
Kinneavy tends to think of audience as a static fact about discourse of a
certain kind, both Moffett and Britton take audience more concretely in
another sense—dynamically, developmentally, the sense of audience unfolding gradually as maturity and experience increase, not in terms solely
of ideal, adult-level competence.

On the development of the sense of audience, Britton moves beyond
Moffett in at least two ways. First, Britton clearly distinguishes between
the audience of orality and the readership of literacy. The distinction is
implicit in Moffett, of course, the I-you scale beginning in oral forms and
ending in publication, but it is comparatively submerged because of Moffett's stress on integrating the verbal arts and his greater emphasis on the
younger student, on the way to literacy but not there yet. With Britton,
however, the distinction is as sharp as it is for Ong; indeed, as noted before,

Britton's concept of readership differs in no essential respects from Ong's "fictive audience," which is arguably the most sophisticated theory of the writer's reader. Britton says explicitly that the writer must create a context of situation (including a reader) that is not actually present. To do so, however, the writer must have experience with the literate universe of discourse, must learn how past writers have fictionalized their readers. Finally, Britton is aware of how difficult the movement from audience to reader is for the child, who may lack both the intellectual ability to sustain fictionalization and the social reinforcement to become truly literate.

The audience-reader distinction, then, is developed to a far greater extent in Britton than it was in Moffett. To Britton's further credit, he does not allow the distinction to become a flat contrast, a hiatus across which the student must somehow leap. Britton would agree with Moffett and Ong that all language use has an oral base, that therefore high-quality discussion nurtures the sense of audience generally. For this reason Britton, like Moffett, questions the closed, teacher-dominated classroom (194–98). And while Britton does not say so explicitly, he would probably also agree with Ong that the difference between audience and reader is ultimately one not of kind but of degree: audiences are never simply just there; even in conversation with intimates, we are speaking to a construct, to our interpretation of someone, with our knowledge of other people being always subject to revision. Consequently, while the differences between speech and writing are significant and full of implications for composition theory and practice, we should avoid the kind of antithetical thinking that would see audience/reader as simply a nonfictive-fictive contrast. Because there are only degrees of abstraction between various kinds of audiences and various kinds of readers, the reader of a personal letter may seem less fictive to the writer than the audience of a public address to a speaker.

The second way that Britton moves beyond Moffett in exploring the sense of audience could scarcely emerge apart from concrete reflection on student writing. I refer to the movement from (according to Britton's creative use of concepts from G. H. Mead) writing for an internalized other versus writing for a generalized other. Any sensitive writing teacher knows intuitively the difference between bright students who are adept at sizing up a teacher and producing what is wanted—writing for the internalized other—and that much smaller group of students who conceive their writing for a genuine reading public, the generalized other. Britton gives this difference very precise formulation. More than that, he discusses the mind-set that aspires to an audience beyond the teacher: it sees in its own work "general value or validity," a "readiness to conform with or contribute to some cultural norm or trend," and "identification with an audience not personal" (72). The transition from internalized other to generalized other, then, is tantamount to maturity, to the ideal readership implicit in our ideal model of the adult aims of discourse. For there is nothing to develop beyond the generalized other; it is the end point of a continuum that has its beginning point in preliterate childhood, in our first conversation—usually with adults and other family members, overwhelmingly not our peers, the first internalized other that children try to manipulate.

What remains, therefore, is tracing in detail the in-between, understanding the stages or phases uncovered both psychologically (in terms of emotional and intellectual growth) and socially (in terms of facilitating conditions), and evolving teaching strategies to promote audience development in the light of our understanding of this much-needed research. In sum, so far as our four theories are concerned, Britton offers the best concepts for investigating audience/reader, especially when combined with Moffett's stronger focus on earlier stages of development. But together they achieve only a first approximation, a definition of what needs to be done.

Britton's theory raises two other issues that should be mentioned here. First, he devotes a chapter to the composing process, without, however, even alluding to rhetoric's traditional divisions of that process—invention, arrangement, and style—the very structuring concepts of D'Angelo's theory. Anyone educated in rhetoric must question the implication of this omission. Was Britton unaware of the rhetorical lore? Or did he judge it irrelevant for some reason? Whatever the answers, Britton's view of the composing process, inspired by Janet Emig (see Britton 21–37), differs strikingly from D'Angelo's rhetorical approach. On the face of it, we seem to have conflicting accounts of the composing process. Are they really complementary? Or do they complement each other in some respects, while conflicting in others? In the next chapter I try to resolve the issue of rhetoric's place within the contemporary view of the writing process.

Second, like Kinneavy, if not precisely for the same reasons, Britton rejects Alexander Bain and George Campbell's "forms of discourse," which Kinneavy overhauled as part of his theory of modes. Unfortunately, Britton rejects not only Bain and Campbell but also the very notion of modality itself on the grounds that it is too prescriptive and too product-oriented. Britton did not see, as Kinneavy did, a useful concept that can be retrieved from the confusing ad hoc Bain-Campbell categories, the concept of discourse means, our basic options for developing what we have to say about any subject. Some notion of modality, I think, is unavoidable, for if we have a typology of ends, aims, or functions, by implication there must also be means for realizing those ends. Furthermore, even if we are oblivious to the terminological pressure of ends implying means and vice versa, modality will creep into our thinking. Thus when Britton appropriates Moffett's I–it relation to develop the informative function, he also lets modality into his theory by the back door, since the I–it relation includes a theory of modes in its progression from chronologic to analogic to tautologic, a theory of modes in everything but name only. And so one may banish the term *means* (or its synonyms), but the concept will still have a submerged presence. Clearly, it is better to bring such ideas to the surface where they can be openly critiqued and systematically elaborated.

If Kinneavy's strength is *conceptual clarity*, the clear and consistent separation of this from that, the kind of thinking that brings a first ordering to any field struggling with unexamined and ambiguous terms—and if Moffett's strength is the opposite of Kinneavy's, tending to undermine any static abstraction, to transform it into a developmental relation so that we see "this" not so much by contrast with "that" but dynamically, as issuing from something else and on the way to realizing a potential that will eventuate in this becoming that—then I would say that Britton's strength lies in accommodating these opposite modes of thought, in a synthesis of opposites. His theory of functions has both static and dynamic dimensions; his theory of audience/reader insists simultaneously on conceptual clarity, on appreciating the differences between speaking and writing, and on developmental relation, since writing is grounded in speaking and since the ability to conceive and adjust to an audience is preparatory to the more demanding task of fictionalizing a reader.

In other words, Britton exemplifies the spirit that animates this study, pointing the way by example to a synthesis of theories. It is mainly his way of thinking about discourse that justifies what I have claimed before: that, on the whole, Britton's theory is an advance on both Kinneavy and Moffett. It is also a product of scrupulous honesty, involving a genuine struggle between raw data and theory, open admission of what it does not know, and a refusal to rush theory into production, into texts and curricular guides. It is a pointing of the way, a study fully deserving its landmark status.

CHAPTER FOUR

D'ANGELO'S THEORY

Overview

A Conceptual Theory of Rhetoric is a "new rhetoric" in a very specific sense. It is not a new rhetoric in Chaim Perelman's meaning, an effort to assert the value of informal reasoning, of ancient dialectic and rhetoric, in the face of Cartesianism (Perelman and Olbrechts-Tyteca 1–4). Nor is it like the many efforts to extend old rhetoric's concept of persuasion to take in the suasive dimension of all language use, as Kenneth Burke's rhetoric of identification (*Rhetoric* xiii–xiv). Rather, D'Angelo's new rhetoric, despite his reverence for the Western rhetorical tradition, is really in the spirit of I. A. Richards, new in the radical sense of "starting over" (3–8, 23–24).

Like Richards, who essentially discards the old rhetoric in favor of a science that would study the nature of misunderstanding and how to overcome it, a kind of practical semantics, D'Angelo wants a rhetorical science, a discipline that would study discourse and discourse processes with the same assumptions and methods that science uses to study any significant phenomenon. More specifically, his theory aims at a science of rhetoric grounded in the science of mind. His interest is the mental processes that govern discovery (invention), arrangement, and style.

In short, theory for D'Angelo means scientific theory. Conceptual means the thought processes behind or underlying language use. About all that remains of the old rhetoric is its divisions, or "offices": invention, arrangement, and style. The fundamental idea of the old rhetoric—art (*techne*), the articulation of principles to guide the production of successful discourse of a certain kind—is no longer fundamental for D'Angelo. Instead, D'Angelo's fundamental idea is that of structure, to which he devotes an entire chapter. The basic assumption is that one can find a relatively stable sameness underlying the shape shifting of history and culture. In discourse, the ground of permanence is biological, at base the common genetic inheritance of the human brain. Because this organ has a structure common to the species, any manifestation of its activity will evince the structure of the brain itself. (Such an idea motivates Lévi-Strauss's analyses of myth and the search in linguistics for a universal grammar, to mention but two of many examples of structuralist thought in the human sciences.)

D'Angelo takes this idea and applies it to rhetoric. The result is that, instead of having three, more or less distinct rhetorical departments, corresponding roughly to stages in the composing process, D'Angelo envisions what might be called a conceptual deep structure, a finite set of thought patterns that structures everything across the board, that is, throughout the composing process and at all levels in the finished discourse. The topoi of invention and the possibilities for formal choices, both at the macro level of arrangement and the micro level of style, are manifestations of the conceptual deep structure, the finite set of basic thought patterns available to mind because, ultimately, they are grounded in brain structure. For D'Angelo the offices of rhetoric are not just related elements but the same process at work at different levels and phases.

The claim for rhetoric as a science goes hand in hand with the structuralist approach; together they compose the central thrust of *A Conceptual Theory*.

D'Angelo also articulates certain key ideas very common in modern rhetorical thought but seldom stated in one place so explicitly. The principal features of his theory, listed in the preface (iv), combined with the propositions central to the theory (27–29), do more than sum up his book; they expose many of the animating ideas of contemporary rhetoric as a whole. Thus while D'Angelo radicalizes one line of thought, pushing structuralism harder than Kinneavy does, he is representative of the audience of college writing teachers he is trying to reach, especially as that audience was when *A Conceptual Theory* appeared, when modern linguistic science, especially Chomsky, seemed to point the way to the promised land.

Analysis

The inclusion of D'Angelo in this study may at first seem arbitrary, since his focus on rhetoric rather than on discourse theory suggests that he ought to be classed with theorists such as W. Ross Winterowd and Richard Young, contributors to new rhetorics centered on the teaching of writing. After all, D'Angelo is not concerned with discourse typologies or discourse development per se, nor does he have a well-developed theory of modes or audiences that would encourage the kind of comparative assessment pursued thus far. Nevertheless, while freely granting that *A Conceptual Theory* cer-

tainly looks different in the context of a Winterowd or a Young, I decided
to include it here for reasons that go beyond its being one of four major
theories produced within a few years of one another, all having a major
impact on the field of composition.

In his suggestions for synthesis, Kinneavy stresses certain categories his
theory shares with Moffett, Britton, and D'Angelo, especially those arising
from the communication triangle ("Pluralistic Synthesis"). To be sure, one
can find the triangular relations in D'Angelo, just as one can dig out a theory
of modes, for example. But the truth is that the triangle plays a very
insignificant role in *A Conceptual Theory*; D'Angelo's categories do not
connect apparently or directly with any of the other three theorists, except
in two areas. He shares the rhetorical offices with Kinneavy; he shares with
Britton an interest in the composing process. Beyond these two specific
connections, one can find, of course, a general spirit of reform and a structuralist mind-set in common, but this attitude or approach is scarcely limited
to our four theorists, nor do they provide a substantial basis for comparative
treatment. There is just not enough categorical overlap between D'Angelo
and the others to justify inclusion on that count alone.

So why, then? For two reasons primarily. First, while it is not hard to
distinguish discourse theory from rhetorical theory, it is also not very prof-
itable. Our discourse theory ought to imply our rhetorical theory and vice
versa, the model in this regard being Aristotle, whose *Rhetoric* melds dispassionate knowledge of actual oratory with normative guidelines for increasing the odds of producing successful oratory on any given occasion.
Unfortunately, none of our theorists comes close to Aristotle's model.
Kinneavy and D'Angelo are the only rhetoricians among our four theorists.
Kinneavy offers a descriptive-cum-normative view of the aims, but no
genuine rhetoric of the aims in Aristotle's concrete, how-to sense; D'Angelo
offers a rhetoric, complete with topoi, patterns of arrangement, and schemes
of style, but no theory of discourse within which this rhetoric should function. The result is strange and unsatisfactory. It is as if, having decided to
become aerialists, we acquired trapezes but no acrobatic instruction, or
acrobatic instruction with no trapezes. Either way the results are not likely
to be happy.

My first reason, then, for taking up D'Angelo is that his study forces us
to address a key question: What notion of rhetoric best complements a
discourse theory designed principally for writing instruction? This and certain other key questions almost demand attention when *A Conceptual Theory*
is considered in the context of discourse theory.

My second reason is that, explicitly or implicitly, D'Angelo poses questions of moment in his own right. For example, fully aware of the history
of rhetoric as an art, he asks if rhetoric could not be a science as well.

Contemporary rhetoric must answer yes; otherwise Kinneavy's theory, clearly scientific in intention, becomes incomprehensible, as does Britton's empirical methodology and hundreds of research projects and reports that obviously assume that discourse and discourse processes can be studied scientifically. A journal such as *Research in the Teaching of English* is founded on an affirmative answer to D'Angelo's question. But if we answer yes, a host of questions follow. What are we doing exactly? Have we created or are we creating a genuine science of literacy, a pure or theoretical discipline that will study discourse, reading, and writing quite as science studies anything else? If so, are we also creating the corresponding technical or applied disciplines? What is the relation of this science of rhetoric, pure and applied, to the traditional art of rhetoric? What is the competent writing teacher to do with all of this in the classroom? And so on.

As in previous chapters, initially the concentration is on our theorist's opening moves, the main concepts he brings into play; from there, we follow the divisions of his book, taking up in order invention, arrangement, and style.

The Basic Concepts

The three theories we have scrutinized thus far have all been two-termed: Kinneavy's aim and mode, Moffett's I-you and I-it, Britton's function and audience. The coherence of D'Angelo's theory likewise depends on two concepts, both of which occur in the title of his book: *rhetoric*, which involves us in distinctions between art and science, between rhetoric and composition; and *conceptual*, which involves us in the relation of language and thought or discourse and mind.

We have already noted that D'Angelo wants a science of rhetoric, a discipline "which attempts to discover general principles of oral or written discourse" and which "subjects its findings and conclusions to close examination and verification." His rhetorician, then, would be a discourse scientist. Composition becomes "the art of applying these principles in writing," the applied or technical counterpart to rhetorical science (3). Presumably, therefore, if we follow D'Angelo we will have two rhetorics: his new one, which will be concerned with discourse in Martin Steinmann's sense of *knowing that*, and will be "systematic, theoretical, and descriptive"; and the old rhetoric, concerned with discourse in Steinmann's sense of *knowing how*, equated with composition and by nature "intuitive, practical, and prescriptive" (2).

If D'Angelo's proposal sounds cogent and reasonable, it probably should, for he is proposing what in fact exists now and what existed in a less developed form when he was writing. Discourse and discourse processes are being studied scientifically; the ancient art of rhetoric, extended quite consciously by revision and supplementation to deal with writing rather than oratory, flourishes in our textbooks and classrooms. And why not? If we can concern ourselves with extinct life forms and black holes, why not with the very medium of scientific knowledge itself? And if we say that writing can be taught, it is hard to see what else we could mean but that composition is to some degree an art, a matter of learning how to make the best choices among the available means for achieving an end.

D'Angelo is not saying, however, that we ought to have two rhetorics, one a science, the other an art, one suited to this, the other to that. His approach is more vertical than that, more in keeping with the pure science-applied technology mode of integration. He is saying that what we learn from a science of discourse ought to be applied directly in the writing courses we teach. He says that this application is an art, but he cannot mean art in Aristotle's sense—an art for Aristotle had no scientific counterpart—rather he must mean art in its more general sense, as when we speak of the art of medicine, concrete practice based on abstract scientific knowledge. In other words, he is really discarding the ancient art of rhetoric, but in a less up-front way than I. A. Richards did.

Again, there is an initial plausibility. Our age is no longer surprised when a subject once thought unconducive to science is added to the sciences. If we can study scientifically something as difficult to access as cognition, why not discourse? And for many, there is almost a categorical imperative here: we ought to study discourse scientifically, for only in this way can we hope to discover whether our subjective impressions match reality. There may be limits to what we can discover about discourse using scientific method, but we ought to push as far as we can go, if only because what we tell our students about discourse should be based on more than traditional lore and rules of thumb.

The problems with D'Angelo's equation of rhetoric with discourse science are not at first apparent. In exposing some of them, especially those closely related to understanding D'Angelo's theory, I am not arguing against the scientific study of discourse. I am, however, arguing against identifying rhetoric with discourse science. Such an equation, as we shall see, makes too few distinctions, cuts us off from the rhetorical tradition, and widens rather than narrows the gap between knowing that and knowing how.

If we intend to reject or ignore the view of rhetoric as an art, we should first see exactly what that view is. Since D'Angelo alludes to Aristotle, we might as well begin with Aristotle's distinctions. The key one is, of course, science as opposed to art, the very distinction D'Angelo discusses. A science has a circumscribed subject matter—politics, biology—and has for its end understanding or explaining the phenomena in question; an art has to do with participating in or creating something, as poems or plays (poetics), speeches (rhetoric), and discussions (dialectic). Since a poem, speech, or discussion might be about virtually anything, the arts have no special subject matter, their end being in any case not to understand or explain some isolatable part of reality per se but rather to understand in order to create poems, deliver speeches, and defend one's side in an argument. And so Aristotle contrasts knack with art, know-how that does not know itself, that cannot explain its own successful performance, with art that can, that makes explicit what is implicit in praxis so far as possible (Cooper 1).

We must reckon, then, with at least two meanings of *knowing that*. A science "knows" when it has verified its descriptions or explanations. An art "knows" when—or, better, doesn't become an art until—it begins to explain itself, until, that is, the tacit knowing of knack becomes to some degree patent. Because D'Angelo does not confront this distinction, he does not see that much that can be known in the scientific sense about discourse has little or no relation to rhetorical art and can do us little good in the writing classroom. Consequently, especially in the chapters on arrangement and style, his theory contributes significantly to description of finished discourses, to the scientific sense of knowing that, but little to the art of making formal and stylistic choices in the act of writing, the rhetorical knowing that. The resulting hiatus is only widened when D'Angelo argues that the primary task of the writing teacher is to convey theory, as if knowing about discourse had a simple and direct correlation with being able to discourse successfully. The genuine foundation of successful writing, however, is not knowing that; it is knack, the mostly unconscious, semi-conscious feel that comes from experience, deep immersion in reading, speaking, and writing. Rhetorical art attempts to build on this know-how by making it more conscious and therefore more reliable and adaptable in circumstances not exactly like those previously experienced—and what rhetorical situation does not have something novel about it? In contrast, science does not build on know-how at all, but abstracts from it: experience may be the source of intuitions, hypotheses, about discourse, but the discourse scientist is concerned with validation and system, with a coherent body of established knowledge about discourse, not with improving the quality of someone's discourse.

In sum, it will not suffice to equate rhetoric with discourse science and contrast it with composition. Rhetoric should retain the meaning it has always had—the art of composition. Rhetoric needs discourse science primarily as a source of reliable typologies for the discourse kinds we intend to teach, each of which needs its own rhetoric. As Aristotle created a rhetoric of oral persuasion, so we need rhetorics for all the aims of written discourse. Beyond that, rhetoric itself should continue to employ scientific methods to test the effectiveness of teaching strategies and should respond to whatever discourse science discovers that is relevant to the art of rhetoric. Thus, there is still a desperate need for the kind of validation used, for example, in sentence combining; and we need to revise continually what we teach in response to the kind of dispassionate study that led to realizing the limitations of Bain's "organic paragraph" model (Stern).

Equating rhetorical art with discourse science will tend to have one of two results, both about equally undesirable: either the science will limit itself to what the art needs to know, or the art will be submerged or lost entirely in the science. Dissociating them in the purist spirit would deprive rhetoric of valuable insight into discourse and cut off the main avenue for bringing science to bear on classroom praxis. Clearly, bringing the two into fruitful relation is the best alternative; judging from the number of people both practicing the art and studying discourse scientifically—the Britton team is an excellent example—the strain of getting the art and the science to work together need not be great. If we can be clear about which hat we are wearing at any particular time and if we can avoid the kind of thinking that promotes science at the expense of art, the way to useful interaction should remain open.

D'Angelo uses the term *concept* as synonymous with *category*. His interest in concept arises from his effort to correlate discourse patterns with thought; hence, "by conceptual patterns of discourse I mean verbal patterns related to thinking activity. These patterns are symbol systems which are objectively distinct from thinking, yet which refer directly to it" (18). By "objectively distinct" he means, of course, that the text or utterance out there is not the same thing as the activity of the mind, the subjective, cognitive processes that produced it. And yet—obviously, somehow—they are closely connected.

Modern rhetoric's fascination with the intellectual processes that make discourse possible arises from the development of psychology and the rejection of the current-traditional paradigm for teaching writing, which concentrated on correctness and form at the expense of invention. Once we turned from product to process, the issue of language and thought had to become salient and urgent. So, to say that D'Angelo is opening an enormous can of worms misses the point; the can was already open and he shows considerable courage in confronting the issue head on.

The problem lies not in what D'Angelo wants to do but rather in his notion of the relation between language and thought. "Thinking does not always manifest itself in symbols," he asserts. "For example, thinking takes place in the act of perception. A person can observe on the perceptual level that one tree is larger than another tree. . . . This kind of thinking does not require verbal symbols" (29). Common sense might agree, but common sense does not recognize the degree to which perception is language permeated. We do not detect the presence of symbols in perception, but they are there nonetheless. To see—perceive—a tree at all *as a tree* is to understand in some fashion the word *tree*. Otherwise, seeing amounts to animal perception, operational but not conceptual; an animal walks around a tree rather than bumps into it, but it does not see a *tree*, since it possesses no label by which it identifies an environmental object. If the human perception of objects depends on names, a relation such as larger than is utterly dependent on language. One cannot just go out and see a "larger than." Such a seeing is a perceiving through language, but at a level so profound that we naturally rebel at the notion that language has anything whatsoever to do with it.

Perhaps D'Angelo is trying to discriminate thought that is verbal from thought that is image. If so, the latter cannot be called nonsymbolic. True, it isn't manifested as verbal symbols. But not only is the mental image tied to language in the deep sense just discussed, it is also itself symbolic. The image represents something: past experience through memory, a present object being meditated, a problem for exploration, or perhaps all at once. Whatever the case, just in being representative the image is a symbol. In this sense, whatever we think when we think the image tree rather than the word tree is every bit as symbolic as any word.

I am not saying that verbal and imagistic thoughts are the same. Clearly the difference is there and it is important for invention. Einstein, for example, depended on "thought experiments"—a form of concrete, image-centered thought—to discover and develop his theories. Evidently neither natural language nor math was any assistance, though the problems he was wrestling with and the solutions he advanced came from and belong to physics, which like all systematic knowledge requires conventional symbols, natural or artificial languages.

There is nothing wrong, then, with D'Angelo's basic intuitions; rather the difficulty lies, first, in how he conceives the general problem of thought and language and, second, arising as a consequence of the first, in how he approaches the relation between discourse out there and the thought that produced it. These matters concern us especially in his chapter on invention; at present, my general point is that any effort to separate thought from language or thought from symbols is probably wasted effort. Lev Vygotsky's basic position is still sound: language and thought arise from different genetic potentials in the brain, but at an early age they merge to the point of inextricability (41–44). The question is not how to relate language to thought but how to relate thought, which is always verbal-symbolic, to speech acts and to texts. The central problem here is the movement from maximally compact thought ("inner speech" for Vygotsky) to the public act of communication, which means not only being sufficiently explicit and conventionally coherent that others may understand but also being adaptable to such variables as situational context.

Beyond this language-saturated view of thought, a conceptual theory must also reckon with the concept of concept itself, especially so far as the development of writing ability is concerned. The presence of language does not necessarily mean the presence of concepts; thought that is verbal–symbolic may not be truly conceptual. If Vygotsky is fundamentally correct, the words of young children are just more or less labels for things; later, children think in congeries or "heaps," an associational (but still not conceptual) mode of thought. Only when they are ready developmentally, and only then when social reinforcement exists, do children begin to use words as genuine concepts (58–69). Conceptual rhetoric's main task is not to resolve the problem of language and thought, best handled by philosophy and psychology, but rather to transform thought that is verbal-symbolic into thought that is conceptual and develop conceptual thought to handle the problems posed by ever more sophisticated writing tasks. Considered in this way, conceptual rhetoric is relevant to all age groups, since conceptual development is never complete; and thought about in this way, we can relate D'Angelo's work directly to the concerns of Moffett and Britton.

The Composing Process

Britton's approach to the composing process combined an Emig-like stage or phase view with phenomenology—concrete reflection on actual acts in the composing process, such as scanning back, rereading what we have already written. The result was a general view coupled with an exploratory attitude. Moffett contributes no notion of the composing process per se; instead, he concentrates on linking other discourse acts, for instance, discussion, with writing, and various forms of writing with each other; the journal, for example, becomes part of the raw material for a historian. One could say that Britton provided an open-ended model and a method for more specific contemplation of the process, while Moffett deals with the whole discursive background of any act of composing.

True to his structuralist approach, D'Angelo defines the problem of composing as "how an intention or purpose that is already partially realized in the mind gets what it needs to complete itself." In this way composing goes on within a part to whole relation, beginning with semantic intent, an initial gestalt, "brought to fulfillment, slowly, bit by bit, by linear methods" (52–53).

While one may question this view on a number of counts—don't we often discover our semantic intent in the process? and aren't our methods as recursive as they are linear?—nevertheless D'Angelo's general view of the composing process is significant for three reasons. First, he sees intent or purpose (synonyms for *aim* in general usage) as incipient rather than as final cause or prime variable (Kinneavy) or as one among many significant variables (Britton). D'Angelo takes a process view of aim, whereas Britton and especially Kinneavy see it primarily as a key notion for explaining or classifying discourse products. Consequently, though without apparently realizing it, D'Angelo answers a question none of our other theorists even pose, a significant question generally passed over in the whole contemporary concern with process: At what point can we say a composing process begins? "With semantic intent" is D'Angelo's answer, for him the same thing as initial gestalt, the projection of the whole, without which the visions and revisions of the rest of the process would lack a center or organizing principle.

D'Angelo's answer is sound, providing that we recognize that the process sometimes begins with a task imposed from without, for which an author must discover a semantic intent; that the initial gestalt can be abandoned or totally transformed in process; and that semantic intent is only the beginning and does not necessarily dictate other choices, such as genre, audience, and format, which may also be beginnings in their own right. D'Angelo's answer is also useful in that contemporary treatments of invention usually fail to distinguish thinking or discovery in general from rhetorical invention proper, which goes on within an initial gestalt, an intuition of the composition as a whole. The notion of semantic intent may help to demarcate the early phases of a sustained discourse act from the matrix of discourse in which it is always embedded. That is, semantic intent strong enough to motivate composing constitutes commitment, an organizing of the energy dispersed into reading, dialogue, note taking, and so on, the constant ongoing immersion in discourse that nurtures rhetorical invention directly and indirectly for all serious writers.

A second level of significance for D'Angelo's view of composing lies in its resemblance to the reading process, itself an act of composition. Like D'Angelo's writer, the reader intuits a whole, including semantic intent, by sampling the text; then, if one actually reads it in the ordinary sense, the initial gestalt is filled in by largely linear methods (though here again rereading, often triggered by the unanticipated, by projections not confirmed by the text, results in recursiveness). Hardly proof of D'Angelo's general view of composing, the fact that reading mirrors his conception of writing at least lends weight to his thesis.

Finally, although D'Angelo's metaphor for the composing process, "a tree whose potential is already partially realized in the seed" (52), should draw little attention in itself, being an organic metaphor typical of our

Romantic inheritance, it does unintentionally reveal the limitations of structure as a metaphor for writing process. D'Angelo actually works with two conflicting images of composing, the spatial gestalt metaphor and the temporal, organic one. The former represents the intellectual habits of structuralism, which wants to characterize everything as a fixed, intuited whole analyzable into complex hierarchies of parts. The traditional outline typifies this way of grasping a composition. The problem, of course, is that writing cannot be characterized simply as a filling in of parts according to a controlling whole. Rather, the actual process involves not only forming but transforming the temporal dimension whereby the structures of the seed (the initial gestalt) undergo radical alterations of form and relation to ultimately produce the tree (the finished composition). But transforming is something structuralism has a hard time embracing with its heuristic images. Structuralism handles best the result of a process or some isolatable stage on the way—hence, D'Angelo's need for the organic metaphor, which he might have exploited better had he worked more consciously with the tensiveness of the structure–organic process metaphors.

Invention

The first problem confronting the would-be analyst of D'Angelo's topics is to discover exactly what they are. On the one hand, they are like Aristotle's topoi in being analytical rather than headings under which to record actual material (e.g., quotations) for later use. On the other hand, they "can be best described as categories which reflect thought processes" (53), suggesting a much broader concern with logic than one finds in Aristotle's *Rhetoric*.

The difficulty cannot be blamed on D'Angelo. The notion of topic has never been clear. It is one of the more vexing interpretative problems connected with Aristotle's *Rhetoric*. And contemporary rhetoric has added much in the way of inventional aids but little in the way of clarification.

Despite the general confusion, however, I think we can confidently assert that, excepting their shared analytical character, D'Angelo's categories have little relation to Aristotle's topoi. The *Rhetoric*'s logical "places" are, first of all, meant as an aid in discovering the available means of persuasion, whereas D'Angelo's categories are not connected to any class or aim of discourse. Furthermore, Aristotle's topoi focus on the generation of enthymemes, on rhetoric's version of deduction, whereas D'Angelo's categories have no such purpose in view (Cooper 5).

Whatever resemblance there may be between Aristotle's list of topics and D'Angelo's (and there is overlap, e.g., definition, partition, analogy), fundamentally they are quite disparate. Nor are there significant parallels between D'Angelo's categories and those found in Aristotle's tract on dialectic, the *Topics*, the source of many of *Rhetoric*'s places. Again, Aristotle has a particular kind of discourse in mind, discussion or argument, and his central aim is to prepare us for the demands of dialectical cross-examination, to play equally well the roles of questioner and responder; his focus is on a particular logical construct, this time the syllogism rather than the enthymeme of rhetoric (Cooper 5). D'Angelo's topoi, then, are not dialectical in Aristotle's understanding of the term.

They are, however, akin to Hegel's categories. Here the likeness is not a mere overlap of terms but shared attitudes, assumptions, and basic distinctions. D'Angelo's topoi are intended to be a partial description of mind, the silent, internal ways of thought, not the collective, give-and-take of the old dialectic, centered on dialogue, conversation. Furthermore, D'Angelo, like Hegel, is interested in mind—intellectual capacity—not in the sort of empirical concern with cognitive development that we found in Britton and especially in Moffett. Finally, in a way very reminiscent of Hegel, D'Angelo conceives his categories as a self-contained system of mutually implied "moments" passing into each other.

Invention always takes place within a system or systems. What is this system like? Paradoxically, the topics of invention are both the parts and the whole of this system. At no stage in the composing process can division into parts be separated from classification or classification from comparison. For D'Angelo, probably all the topics operate together as a single entity in the process of composing (53).

Of course, I am claiming only a family resemblance. D'Angelo's topoi are also not like Hegel's in many respects; for example, D'Angelo does not deduce them from a single category in a sequence held necessary or compelling. Nevertheless, D'Angelo's topics are dialectical in a mainstream modern sense: logic as the mind's system.

In calling them dialectical, however, we have only a label. What follows from this status? Most important, in being dialectical they are not truly rhetorical topics at all. D'Angelo is correct in saying that invention "always takes place within a system or systems," since someone must invent or discover, and the mind depends on brain and social systems. But rhetorical invention has more than thought itself as a context. It aims at discourse of a certain kind, for a certain audience or readership, working within concrete limitations of time or space and almost always with some conception of the medium of publication. There is a difference between dialectical invention, whether sustained by solo thought or conversation, and rhetorical invention, whose thrust is "to discover the available means" to sustain an extended oral or written monologue.

D'Angelo is scarcely alone in failing to distinguish invention in general from rhetorical invention in particular—indeed, no contributor to the contemporary revival of interest in invention has done so. The reasons are complex: inattention to Aristotle's distinction between dialectic and rhetoric, the transformation of dialectic itself by German idealism, the expansion of rhetoric to handle all written discourse, which detached it from the aim of persuasion and from aim-centeredness generally. But the results are relatively simple and predictable: richness of inventional resources, poverty of selective principles. We have a wealth of heuristics to stimulate thought but little guidance in selecting only what is appropriate for the demands of a particular discourse act—*this* purpose, readership, set of external constraints, medium of publication, and so on.

The judgment, taste, and tact governing selection of means—from what to say to how to say it—is, of course, the art of rhetoric, an art because no algorithm or heuristic can reliably control or predict our choices in any given case; each given case is to some degree unique. In seeking a science of rhetoric, D'Angelo neglects this whole dimension of rhetoric as an art. In pursuing the implications of what he calls conceptual rhetoric, he has actually produced a system of thought categories (the adjective *conceptual* is certainly justified), not thought disciplined by or channeled into the needs of discourse acts—for *rhetoric*, then, read *dialectic*. Dialectic, whether old or new, after Aristotle or after Hegel, is nothing if not conceptual; we ought therefore to eliminate the tautology and translate *conceptual rhetoric* simply as "dialectic."

Understood in this way, D'Angelo's contribution is significant on a number of counts. First, he rescues the traditional topoi from the pathetic state into which they had fallen in too many texts and handbooks, where they were treated as types or methods of paragraph development rather than what they truly are, intellectual places, names for thought operations. Second, instead of offering a mere collection of topics—as Aristotle does—D'Angelo gives us a system, an organized hierarchy of topics; this not only makes them easier to remember but also suggests relations among the topics not readily detectable in a listing (42–43). Third, while D'Angelo's topoi are hardly his, original and interesting touches go into his organization of them. For instance, we are familiar with the terminology "static, progressive, and repetitive" as the major divisions of Kenneth Burke's treatment of form. D'Angelo uses these divisions, however, as the first level of division for his logical topics (105–07), where they function well in an unexpected context. Finally, D'Angelo's effort to join the ancient topical tradition to the concerns of written composition connects with the work of other rhetoricians, such as Chaim Perelman, who consciously draws from Aristotle's dialectic in his search for the "places" used in philosophical writing (Perelman and Olbrechts-Tyteca 5).

This last point suggests that D'Angelo is on the right track, even if his treatment of invention confuses rhetoric with dialectic and neglects rhetorical art almost completely. This right track links the development of intricate, sophisticated thought with literacy and written composition. As Eric Havelock and Walter Ong have shown, dialectic at its origin, despite its reliance on the oral medium of dialogue, is the creation of a literate mentality (Havelock, *Preface* 197–233; Ong, *Orality* 80–81). The analytical habits of dialectic make it more nearly akin to writing than to oratory, to rhetoric "old style." Our rhetoric—the art of written composition—demands the dialectician's art. In large measure what we mean when we complain that our students can't (or don't) think is that they lack the art of verbal analysis once fostered by dialectical training.

In focusing on the conceptual underpinnings of discourse, then, D'Angelo is certainly pursuing something significant. Further progress depends on a full, conscious revival of dialectic, coupled with clear recognition of the difference between dialectical invention, limited in theory only by the mind's capacity, and rhetorical invention, limited by aim, readership, constraints of time or space, mode of publication, and the like.

The Notion of Nonlogical Topic

A legacy of nineteenth-century scholarship is the recovery of classical rhetoric, especially Aristotle, whose tracts on the verbal arts had little direct impact before our own century. Aristotle, of course, is the origin of philosophical rhetoric, what George A. Kennedy calls primary rhetoric, distinguished by its stress on logos and on composition as the conscious process of selection guided by explicit knowledge of the art (41–85). While invaluable, especially in its encouragement of theoretical rigor, philosophical rhetoric has also a strong and potentially disabling bias against full appreciation of the a- or nonlogical processes of invention. This bias clashes with contemporary awareness of the mind as relatively more unconscious or nonconscious than conscious. In short, depth psychology, brain research, studies of creativity, and such key notions as Polanyi's "tacit knowledge" all suggest that primary rhetoric's approach to invention cannot be adequate.

And yet, while everyone knows that the process of discovery cannot be reduced to logical analysis or conscious art, by far the greater portion of contemporary efforts to nurture invention continue to work in the vein of primary rhetoric. This is so because the very idea of teaching invention entails conscious, deliberate intervention in the composing process; because even so-called right-brain thinking normally involves making sense of the results of such thought, which means conceptual formulation and analysis; and because it is difficult to tap into or trigger the immense energy of the unconscious mind. It is therefore not surprising that D'Angelo may be the only rhetorical theorist to allot a systematic place to both logical and non-logical topics in his theory of invention (47–52). More than anything else, in fact, his effort to treat both together without prejudice probably consti-tutes his most original contribution to rhetoric's first office.

Two problems, however, beset his treatment. First, the dichotomy logi-cal–nonlogical is unfortunate. Logic itself, needless to say, is a notoriously elusive concept, but no matter how one delimits it, logic has never excluded the nonlogical from its midst. We have not only the leap of induction but also the premises, assumptions, or axioms at the head of every deductive process, which cannot themselves be deduced and which can only be intuited somehow and accepted. As for the logic of the nonlogical: two of D'An-gelo's nonlogical topics, condensation and displacement, were originally advanced to explain the logic of dreams, while a third, free association, supposedly reveals the inner coherence, the logic of personal semantics, the idiosyncratic meanings individuals attach to public symbols (Strachey 527–32).

Instead of speaking of logical versus nonlogical, we would be better off to speak of explicit-implicit, the formulated–not yet formulated; while doubtless there are modes of discovery and expression that elude full ver-balization, only the articulate or potentially articulate ones matter for rhet-oric and composition.

The second problem is that the kind of discovery that D'Angelo has in mind when he refers to the nonlogical contradicts the meaning of topic itself. *Nonlogical topic* is a contradiction in terms. The very nature of topoi is to be at hand, available as any heuristic is available, simply by calling it to mind, centering one's attention on one place at a time. We can therefore exhort someone to define x. Or we can pose a question drawn from a topos, such as, To what class does x belong? The nonlogical cannot be approached this way. It is not at hand. It is absurd to command someone to go dream. That person *will* dream; these dreams will spontaneously use condensation and displacement. All we can do where the nonlogical is concerned is cul-tivate receptiveness (dreams, for example, come most readily when they are treated as a welcome guest), encourage serious attention to the results of imagination in all its forms, and engage our students in activities, such as free association, that will tell them that it is not only acceptable to make such processes part of invention but positively desirable to do so.

As I noted before, D'Angelo's instincts are sound. We cannot regard invention as only a conscious, deliberate process, dismissing the other di-mension as something that will take care of itself. It is clear that the non-logical can be developed and that the attitudes of teachers toward what is misleadingly labeled creativity (as if conceptual thought and even formal logic cannot be creative) do make a difference. But it is not helpful to treat this other dimension as if it were reducible to a topical system. Topoi can be applied to analyze, say, a dream or the results of free association, but D'Angelo's entire list of nonlogical topics are not really topics at all, nor can any topical system characterize or bring into play the pre- or nonconceptual. Rather, this dimension must be approached with Moffett-like indirection, through classroom activities designed to encourage and sanction so-called creative thinking.

Arrangement

D'Angelo begins his treatment of rhetoric's second office where most serious, contemporary theorizing begins—in dissatisfaction with traditional lore. The vacuous observation that discourses have "a beginning, middle, and an end" is dismissed as "almost worthless." The "patterns of development" approach, once standard in composition textbooks, is "usually superficial." Finally, classical arrangement's concern with the parts of an oration (*exordium, narratio, confirmatio,* etc.) seems "too mechanical, static, and arbitrary" and too limited by the norms of oral persuasion (55, 56).

Having thus rejected traditional approaches to arrangement, D'Angelo advances a threefold program of his own. First, he transforms his topoi for invention into patterns for arrangement, attempting to follow through on his systematic assumption that invention, arrangement, and style exemplify the same underlying "forms of the mind" (57–59). Second, in chapter 5, he explains and demonstrates what he calls syntagmatic structure, basically his "generative rhetoric of the essay," which extends Francis Christensen's generative rhetoric of the paragraph to encompass an entire discourse. And third, in chapter 6 he complements syntagmatic with its opposite, paradigmatic, which amounts to applying to discourse a method of analysis similar to the one developed by Claude Lévi-Strauss and others for the analysis of myth.

It is revealing that D'Angelo does not attempt to follow through on his notion that topoi are also mutatis mutandis, forms of arrangement. He says that they are, outlines them as such, but then shifts attention entirely to discourse analysis, to syntagmatic and paradigmatic treatments of several actual discourses, leaving the topoi or forms behind. Why? What exactly is happening here?

First, I think it likely that D'Angelo sensed the inadequacy of his own hypothesis, his effort to equate invention, arrangement, and style. It is true, of course, that some of the topoi are also principles of *dispositio* as well as schemes of style. Analogy is a clear example: a fertile analogy is often the best fruit of invention; analogies have structured whole books and essays and parts of both; and we have all paused to admire the striking, local use of analogy on the stylistic level, the brilliant comparison that occupies a phrase or a sentence. It is also true, however, that some topics are not so ubiquitous. Cause and effect, for instance, a topic of ancient lineage, certainly is a structural principle but not a feature of style. Conversely, there are in D'Angelo's list categories with strong structural implications, such as narrative, which seem dubious both as topics and as stylistic elements. I suggest that D'Angelo does not work out his thesis in detail because the topics of invention and the patterns of arrangement are really not the same. Even if they were, it is difficult to see how such knowledge would help a writer. Knowing, for example, that analogy can function formally does not tell me how to develop one or whether to use a particular analogy for a particular purpose, audience, or occasion.

If it is true that classical rhetoric treats its offices in too lockstep a manner, as if they were totally discrete and altogether different, it is also true that D'Angelo's effort to overcome their dissociation from one another by virtually equating them oversimplifies as well. There is doubtless a large measure of overlap. But if they were identical or even nearly so, we would not have students with good ideas and poorly organized papers. And D'Angelo would not require almost two chapters of syntagmatic and paradigmatic analysis, neither of which is derived or can be derived from the topics turned patterns.

What ought we to conclude about D'Angelo's hypothesis that invention, arrangement, and style all result from the same underlying process? There must be some truth here: the same mind invents and organizes. Furthermore, to invent is to form; "formless content" is an unreal abstraction; therefore, invention and arrangement are the same. But they are also different. The acts of discovery belong mainly to inner speech and dialogue, individual thought and discussion. They come to us arranged already, but in the highly compact, mostly implicit way of thought and good talk among friends. The formed must be further formed, elaborated, illustrated, turned into complete propositions linked to other propositions if a speech or a written discourse is to result. Arrangement, then, and style as well, actually designate the movement from the restricted code of inner speech to the elaborated code of a talk or an article—from self-communication, limited only by the quality of one's mind and the present loci of thought, to communication with mostly unknown others, limited much more severely by communicative conventions. Invention and arrangement, therefore, are clearly not the same.

In sum, the offices of rhetoric are best conceived as "identities-in-difference" (Hegel 516), the same and not the same. Only with this understanding

can we achieve the complex awareness required to avoid either departmentalizing them or reducing them to empty identity.

Turning briefly to the real focus of D'Angelo's work on arrangement,
syntagmatic and paradigmatic structure, we should note, first, that his justification for both kinds of analysis is their contribution to formal awareness.
The assumption, unfortunately a secure one, is that most composition students at all levels lack any detailed understanding of prose structure. So
D'Angelo proposes that we reveal prose structure in two ways. First, there
is surface structure, the province of syntagmatic analysis, which shows that
the sections or paragraphs of discourse relate to one another by coordination
and subordination, the same relations that structure sentences. The result
is an essay diagram, a large-scale version of Christiensen's familiar diagrams
of paragraphs and cumulative sentences. Second, there is deep structure,
the province of paradigmatic analysis, which attempts to abstract away from
both what is said and the sentence-to-sentence structure of the discourse to
the underlying basic plan from which the structure was generated. For
example, many a stretch of prose begins with a general claim developed
and confirmed by a string of illustrative examples and concluded by a
restatement of the claim itself.

Clearly D'Angelo's intent is to disengage students from the appearance
that prose has for nearly everyone untrained in discourse analysis—a blank
homogeneity, full of meaning perhaps, but otherwise opaque. They see
little to nothing structurally because no one has shown them the hierarchical
organization of prose from the sentence level on up, or the basic formal
tactic or plan or intent that a writer followed but that is hardly visible to
those for whom prose is an invisible carrier of meaning only.

As with any relatively concrete treatment of arrangement, D'Angelo's
can be easily called into question. The idea, for instance, that essays can be
handled as macroparagraphs constitutes, at best, a highly oversimplified
first approximation of the complexities of structure at the whole discourse
level; to make it work, one must choose one's examples carefully. Nevertheless, D'Angelo's methods will help to create the formal awareness he is
after, and a first approximation is better than none, or better than vague
talk about "flow," or better than simply ignoring the problem of arrangement altogether for lack of a handle on it. And beyond any doubt, what
D'Angelo offered is still much better than the hapless "conventional wisdom" of the vast majority of our textbooks produced since *A Conceptual
Theory* appeared.

At the same time, no matter how useful syntagmatic and paradigmatic
analyses may be, they have at least two significant shortcomings, both
stemming from the scientific-structuralist bent of D'Angelo's entire theory.

As *Cohesion in English* has shown us in detail, structure is only one dimension of arrangement, the other being the various means of cohesion—noun equivalence chains, for example, which are at most only weakly hierarchical (Halliday and Hasan 1–30). This linear dimension of connectedness and transitional devices is not illuminated by structural modes of thought, so it is scarcely surprising that D'Angelo has little to say about it. There is also the obvious fact that, while discourse analysis, being an analysis of products, may aid with formal awareness in general, it does not purport to handle formal choices in process at all. From this angle, for all the abstractness of classical arrangement, we see that it did provide a rough-and-ready means of disposing the results of invention. The ancient art of rhetoric, then, is on this and other counts much closer to writing as a process than is the modern structuralism of both Kinneavy and D'Angelo.

Style

D'Angelo's treatment of style (ch. 7) offers little that is new, serving rather to confirm and extend the thinking exemplified in the whole theory. Since by now the major features of his thought should be clear, my comments can be less elaborate.

Since Benedetto Croce, it has not been acceptable to speak of style as ornament, as decor added to function or message, or as clothing, the outward dress of something more substantial, the body or content of the discourse. Dichotomies like substance and form, content and style, what to say and how to say it are out of fashion. Thus, when D'Angelo claims that style "is not the mere embellishment of a more stable quality in discourse " (104), few would dissent.

Moreover, it is now common among both literary critics and rhetoricians to view the structure-style distinction as arbitrary, a mere analytical convenience. And so "style in the theory of conceptual rhetoric is inseparable from form," D'Angelo tells us, adding a few pages later that "the idea of style as structure conceives of style as the totality of an extended discourse" (109). Style equals structure equals the whole discourse.

Hegel's notion of identity in difference applies as much to these equations as it did in the last section to the identification of invention and arrangement. As there, D'Angelo has part of the truth here. Clearly every stylistic choice is a structural choice; one cannot alter even a single word in a composition without minutely affecting part-whole relations in the totality of an extended discourse. Furthermore, a writer's sense of the totality conditions all choices made in the process of drafting ("at the point of utterance," in Britton's phrase) and in the process of editing; totality, D'Angelo indicates, exists first as a projected whole and then as an actuality when a draft is completed, the whole within which redrafting and editing transpire.

D'Angelo's equations illuminate both product and process views of discourse, despite the pull of structuralism toward the former, toward discourse as an object for analysis. However, any assertion of identity (apart from abstract self-identity, A is A) conceals differences, lost if the dialectic of identity in difference is not pursued. At an abstract level D'Angelo is right to say that metaphor may appear at the local level, as part of what used to be called texture, or more pervasively as a conceit, an extended metaphor for developing whole discourses and parts of discourses. In this sense the same process is at work at different levels, as D'Angelo maintains. But viewed more concretely, in terms of the actual process of choosing, the arbitrary distinction between style and arrangement is anything but a mere analytical convenience. Having "discovered" a metaphor (or do metaphors find us?), we must somehow decide whether to use it as a single isolated thrust, a brief spotlight on our material, or to develop it more systematically as a steady and general light. Immediately we see that the two possibilities are far from the same process. Choosing the latter entails a host of further choices, while the former requires little more than deciding exactly the form of expression and the place of deployment.

We may further observe that our choice is conditioned by a good deal more than our projected sense of the whole. How the metaphor strikes us, its revealing power, governs in large measure what use we can make of it; it will make demands on us also, compelling us along certain lines, and perhaps bringing us into conflict with other variables, such as a readership that wants an explicit argument rather than the suggestive expansiveness of implied comparison.

My point is that composition is not the harmonious fitting of parts to whole that the structural analogy suggests. It is, rather, highly conflictual, impulse countering impulse, going on most often in earlier drafts not within a totality but within a developing sense of various possible totalities, as decision leads to decision. We must also recognize that a discourse need not be a whole in D'Angelo's sense, a hierarchical integration of parts. As we have learned to appreciate the un-well-made poem, so the un-well-made essay is no longer an alien notion but almost a norm in certain circles, one that eludes reduction to whole or totality altogether and yet is scarcely nonlogical in D'Angelo's sense either.

Enough has been said, I hope, to indicate that the more concretely one ponders D'Angelo's equations, the more they cease to equate. The premise that style equals structure equals the total discourse is most convincing when the finished discourse is viewed as an object out there, treated with the psychic distance of the analyst. D'Angelo's equations do not capture the struggle to compose and may even imply a model of composing at variance with felt experience.

I have only a few comments to make about the rest of D'Angelo's chapter on style. Discourse analysis is its main business, justifiable for the same reason that his syntagmatic-paradigmatic analyses were justifiable—as an aid to prose awareness, this time on the more local level of style. It is worth emphasizing that such a concern is fully justified, since many composition teachers, though perhaps skilled in analyzing poetry, drama, or literary prose, see little in scientific or persuasive prose. That is one reason they teach only the content of essays in freshman English anthologies. It is regrettable, therefore, that D'Angelo chose a passage from Thomas Wolfe's novel *You Can't Go Home Again* as his only text for analysis. While the text itself is rich and the analysis skillful, the choice reinforces a widespread prejudice held even by those too well informed to affirm it in so many words: that studying "real style" in writing means turning to literary examples. We need to concentrate on style in nonliterary prose, where it is most invisible to teacher and student alike.

Conclusion

The following statements summarize my assessment of *A Conceptual Theory of Rhetoric*:

1. *Rhetoric as science*. Rhetorical processes can be usefully studied using scientific assumptions and methods. But rhetoric itself is an art.
2. *Structuralism*. Useful analytically and typologically, the structural metaphor fails to illuminate writing as a process and rhetoric as an art.
3. *Conceptual rhetoric*. As applied to invention, conceptual rhetoric deals with thought processes generally, apart from rhetorical variables. As such, it prompts solo thought or dialogue—dialectic, not rhetoric.
4. *Equivalence of rhetorical offices*. The notion of equivalence effectively counters any overly rigid separation of invention, arrangement, and style, while revealing important relations among them. But the offices are better handled through the dialectic implicit in identity in difference.

D'Angelo's version of "new rhetoric" is not the new rhetoric to work hand-in-hand with discourse theory. What we need is not a new rhetoric but new rhetorics—rhetorics that will formulate the art-of-the-discourse types our discourse theories discriminate or, minimally, rhetorics for the kind of writing we intend to teach. Efforts in this direction have been made in Kinneavy, McCleary, and Nakadate's text; in *Four Worlds of Writing* (Lauer et al.); and in numerous texts that concentrate on a single aim of discourse, as in technical writing. But this task is just beginning and will not go very far without a reasonably stable theory of discourse and a resolve to follow through on what we all know, that rhetoric is no longer a single, unified art but many arts.

PART TWO

A DIALOGICAL SYNTHESIS— AND BEYOND

CHAPTER FIVE

PRELIMINARIES

Our focus now changes from the theories in their particularity to a theory drawing from all four, from relatively detailed assessment to a synthesis that largely assumes the ground already covered. But before a synthesis can begin, its suppositional framework requires some explication. Accordingly, I want to explain what I mean by *dialogical* and by *synthesis*; and I want to pose a question that has no obvious answer in our field: What should a theory of discourse do?

Following these preliminaries, I turn to the synthesis, beginning with the two essential notions *multidimensionality* and *dialectic*. The synthesis itself takes shape around nine variables, all in my view necessary to an understanding of any discourse, whether seen as product or process, structurally or dynamically.

The Dialogical Attitude and Method

One of the more influential books to appear in the second half of our century is Thomas Kuhn's *Structure of Scientific Revolutions*. This work made salient the concept of paradigm and stimulated calls, including my own "Brief Plea," for a paradigm to guide thought, research, and teaching in rhetoric and composition.

Reluctantly I have come to feel that no paradigm will ever materialize in our field. We have, of course, a broad consensus among true professionals that might qualify, loosely speaking, as a philosophy—one that defines itself by contrast, for instance, with the current-traditional paradigm (Fogarty 118) and that is commonly sloganized as the "process approach" to writing. But this broad consensus is scarcely a paradigm in Kuhn's sense of the term: an explanation that accounts for all significant knowledge in a scientific field and has drawn the provisional assent of all (or very nearly all) researchers working in the field. Press our broad consensus hard, and assent vanishes; the highly specific and detailed theory that Einstein provided for physics and Darwin for biology simply does not exist for rhetoric and composition.

Furthermore, I think it cannot exist. Kuhn distinguished fields that evolve from fields that undergo periodic revolutions (160–73). However questionable this distinction might be, rhetoric is surely an evolutionary field. We define ourselves by reference to the past. The turn from the product orientation of the recent past, while releasing something akin to the energy and excitement that attends revolutions, was largely a return to our roots. We rediscovered the process view of classical rhetoric. Our "new rhetorics," like those of Chaim Perelman and Kenneth Burke, were usually revisions or extensions of the old. Kinneavy is typical: *A Theory of Discourse* amounts finally to a reassertion of the liberal arts tradition, the heir of *paideia*. And even D'Angelo, whose view of rhetoric as a science has revolutionary potential, presents his theory in the context of classical rhetoric.

The truth is that rhetoric has never had more than a broad consensus; rhetorical thought is normally paradigmless and conflictual. It has been so since Plato attacked the Sophists and Aristotle tried to combine aspects of both views. Rhetoric periodically rediscovers itself, but never really discards a past view in the sense that Copernicus replaced Ptolemy or Einstein, Newton. Our attitude here does not matter at all. We must come to terms somehow with what we have—a field that will never have the degree of internal coherence of those guided by paradigms.

How can we respond most constructively to this 2,500-year-old situation? With a dialogical attitude and method and a dialectical effort to accommodate opposites.

Dialogical attitude is perhaps most quickly grasped by contrast with other attitudes. (I discuss dialectical effort later as one of the two key ideas guiding my synthesis.) Faced by a host of contending voices, of many theories appealing for assent, the basic stances are few. We can say, "A pox on all your houses," and simply practice rhetoric by the light of intuition and experience. If the former is sound and the latter extensive, such a stance may work very well, but any way of practicing rhetoric at least implies a theory. This stance finally amounts to a refusal to articulate theory, not theorylessness. The stance that begins with the curse can take as well the Cartesian turn: clean house, start over. While always tempting, such a choice almost always results in the reinvention of the wheel, failure to recruit followers, or the addition of merely another voice to the existing contention.

And then there is the attitude I call happy eclecticism, probably the second most common after indifference to theory. Its strength is openness, its weakness a refusal to construct a consistent viewpoint, to push ideas hard enough to create the positive tension of creative thought.

Finally, there is the "camp strategy," which takes one of two forms: it either enlists in an existing "school" of thought (e.g., prewriting, tagmemics), or it sets out to create its own camp, typically by emphasizing one strand in the Western rhetorical tradition. Either route has the advantage of a firm identity amid the chaos of theories; the disadvantage is that identity is usually achieved at the price of one-sidedness, for the camp follower or maker ignores or rejects insight from other sources that cannot be assimilated to the party line.

Dialogics resembles eclecticism in its attitude: a welcoming of all constructive voices. But its method is not eclecticism's grocery-cart approach of selecting whatever happens to appeal or meet a present need without regard for the total picture. Instead of accepting even contradictory formulations, dialogics seeks to create the positive tension necessary for theoretical development by a method of relentless questioning. In striving most of all to get competing theories to "talk" to one another, the dialogic strategy threatens the monologuist, whether of the "school" variety or the more athletic from-the-ground-up tactics of Descartes.

What I attempted to do in the previous four chapters (no doubt imperfectly) was to converse with our four theorists, countering them sometimes with my own voice, sometimes with each other, but always with one goal in mind—to find the best in each theory out of which to make my synthesis. Before I discuss synthesis I would like to clarify further my attitude toward *dialogics*.

Walter Ong has said that dialogics has become almost faddish (*Presence* 293). Given the international situation, it is not hard to see why, since the choice would seem to be either mutual accommodation or mutual destruction. Hence, the absolute value attributed to dialogue: "at least they are talking to each other" is the journalist's cliché, heard at least once every time there is a summit between the Soviet Union and the United States.

Talking—even eristic talking—is certainly preferable to fighting, and dialogue may have an absolute value in that it is difficult to attribute more than an abstract humanity to anybody one has not talked to or cannot talk to. Where the issue, however, amounts to a will to power, one may doubt the efficaciousness of dialogue quite as much as one may not attempt to engage the totally convinced. At any rate, dialogics—its method and attitude—has not for me any magical power; I see it simply as best adapted to conditions in rhetorical theory. We have no paradigm and no realistic hope of producing one. What we have is dialogics in the form of theoretical controversy; what we need is a winnowing process, for which dialogics is the best instrument.

The Notion of Synthesis

The Greek word *synthesis* means "seeing together." The term covers roughly three kinds of seeing together, to which I have given the names loose, literal, and creative.

A loose synthesis is like a seashell collection. Separate items are brought together, each having about equal interest and weight, to form a whole only in the sense of a temporary combination of discrete components. Remarking on the work of a mutual friend and colleague, a colleague of mine commented, "His idea of a synthesis is to put disparate materials between the covers of a single book." That is what I mean by loose synthesis; the eclectic strategy discussed above produces them.

Literal syntheses, on the other hand, are as obsessed with vertical integration as loose syntheses are careless of it. In this view, a genuine synthesis must discard nothing and merge everything point by point. If really pushed hard, such an attitude makes synthesis quite impossible, for no two theories can finally be reduced to simple identity, total merger without distinction. In practice, however, the literal synthesis avoids the reduction to absurdity by reducing difference to "a green thought in a green shade"—by, in other words, moving to a vocabulary more abstract than the theories being synthesized. The result is conceptual integration, satisfying in its own way, but with a loss of specifics, of detail.

Surely there is something better than all parts and no whole or all-encompassing vacuity, something better than no rigor or a self-defeating overrigorousness. The something better is a creative synthesis, closely akin as I think of it to the kind of synthesis Hegel espoused.

The creative synthesis is a critical synthesis, and thus different from both the loose and the literal in this respect. Not all theories are worth preserving; some parts of all theories are false leads or are self-limited in ways that demand overcoming. Hence, the winnowing process I referred to in the last section, accomplished by what Burke calls the "ongoing conversation" of history (*Philosophy* 110–11). The theory that fails to shed a sustaining light drops out of the dialogic process; those aspects of still vital theories that are no longer vital get no play, no voice. Sometimes the process requires hastening, in accord with Nietzsche's maxim that what is about to fall ought to be pushed; sometimes the process needs most of all to recover kinds of thinking lost that changed circumstances require again. The critical process, of course, is scarcely foolproof—not, alas, as Hegel thought, inevitable, necessary, progressing toward the ever better and finally a best. There is no closure, only dialogics. But the point is that a creative synthesis is critical—not a shell collection and not a mechanical merger of past systems.

A creative synthesis also assumes that the truth is the whole, which means in practice two things. First, any field of study, despite appearances, really is coherent and evolves—perhaps not smoothly and certainly not without periods of decay and getting off track—toward more adequate, more precise, more workable formulations (without, however, actually getting there in the sense of ultimate closure). Such an assumption is purely an article of faith, part of William James's "will to believe." But without it, theory and metatheory lose point and energy.

Second, if the truth is the whole, it follows that we will have to accommodate disparate and contradictory "truths." "The whole" is the motivating telos of theoretical work, not something actually attainable by finite theories produced by historical individuals. Consequently, after the work of dialogics comes the work of synthesis, fitting together what survives critique, the test of time. Where the partial truths of theories simply diverge, synthesis requires only locating the insights of each within a more embracing framework, one that is less partial, closer to the whole. But if partial truths seem to or do contradict one another, synthesis requires greater tact and ability to accommodate. Some contradictions are only apparent, dissolving under scrutiny into statements about different objects or processes. But even here, detecting and explaining the apparentness of a contradiction can be a first-order challenge.

Some contradictions, however, are just what they seem to be, contradictions. Traditional logic says that if statements *a* and *b* are contradictory, one of three possibilities must obtain: *a* is true and *b* is false; *a* is false and *b* is true; or both are false. But dialectical logic tries to preserve both statements as partial truths, perhaps by seeing them as true at different points in a process or from differing points of view at the same point. For example, D'Angelo's view of the primary task of writing teachers contradicts Moffett's, the former holding that their job is to teach theory, the latter holding that theories are for teachers and should guide the main responsibility, stage-managing a dramatic classroom busy with discoursing, not talking about discourse. Both views are justifiable, but at different times in student development. Younger students will most likely not understand theoretical abstractions or be able to apply them. But with the onset of formal operations, students do increasingly need theory to bring to fuller consciousness their own half-articulated notions and to question ideas they have acquired from a too limited experience or from the quirks of a teacher.

Not all contradictions can be accommodated as easily as this one. The point is that a creative synthesis does something that the literal synthesis normally eschews as illogical: accommodation of contradictory insights.

Like all serious theorizing, a creative synthesis of theories is a venturing beyond established wisdom and "safe" positions. It has structure: centrally, the tension between maximum horizontal inclusiveness and maximum vertical integration. It has method: critique and accommodation. But none of this saves the creative synthesis from error or rebuttal. Some will critique the critiques. Others will find or think they have found a better synthesis. In any case, the whole will gracefully elude even the best synthesis. The goal is appreciable advance, movement of the dialogue, if only a small step, beyond where it was.

What Should a Theory of Discourse Do?

Some readers may feel that I should have asked what a theory of discourse should do long ago, perhaps as early as the introduction. If I had, the answer might have made analysis of the four theories more efficient. It seemed preferable, however, to see first what they actually did.

At a minimum, if we judge from what our theories try to do, an adequate theory of discourse for rhetoric and composition must do the following:

1. Establish a universal typology, capable of classifying all instances of discourse, past, present, and even future.
2. Isolate the norms for each discourse type: typical logic, tactics of arrangement, style.
3. Create a modal theory, the universal means of discourse development.
4. Postulate a learning sequence, kindergarten through twelfth grade, presumably the basis for learning sequences in college. This learning sequence must integrate all the language arts, not attend just to writing, and do so in a way that is consistent with intellectual and emotional development.
5. Understand how people actually compose.
6. Erect a theory of readerships and writer's attitudes (stance, tone).
7. Develop a rhetorical theory that accounts for the act of writing in toto, including all mental processes related to it.

Note that this modest list of only seven items merely sets down what the theories we have examined envisioned as goals. Any reasonably imaginative student of rhetoric could add at length to this wish list. For instance, a theory of discourse ought to be able to account for the history of discourse, which would add a cultural-social dimension to the formal, processual, and psychological dimensions dominant in the seven-item list.

My basic point is a simple one: we ask too much of our theories. What does this statement mean exactly?

Part of our "theoretical problem" is self-engendered. We have sometimes set either impossible goals or goals that cannot be attained by theoretical effort alone. Kinneavy's universal typology exemplifies impossible goals and Moffett's learning sequence unattainable ones. We can reasonably hope for a model of discourse purposes. However, as one theorist put it, the relation between purpose and form in discourse is asymmetrical (Beale 17–21), which means that we will never be able to predict the features of a discourse from knowledge of purpose alone—not even "typical" patterns of logic, arrangement, and style. At best, we can employ Kinneavy's aim typology to group discourse genres in use at a particular time and place; study of the genres themselves will be required to isolate normative features. Similarly, no learning sequence is possible without extensive empirical research. Of course, the job of theory is to account for what is known and to extrapolate therefrom to produce fruitful hypotheses for research. But we only spin our wheels when we attempt what cannot be done.

If part of the theoretical problem is of our own making and hence capable of melioration, most of it derives from the nature of our field and must simply be lived with as cheerfully as possible. For many reasons the field of rhetoric and composition does not have and probably will never have a paradigm in the strict sense of the word. One reason is the sheer breadth and complexity of the field. No theory belonging to one of the special sciences would be called on to account for as much as our theories routinely engage. We have no well-defined chunk of reality for our object of study. Account for the act of writing? Surely we must, but that means not only a theory of discourse and rhetorical arts for each discourse kind but also an understanding of cognition, which means drawing on a host of sciences, including neural physiology, developmental psychology, sociology of knowledge, and so on. Even if we could synthesize such vast reservoirs of knowledge, we have only just begun. For noncognitive processes play a sizable role in writing, and we cannot understand writing apart from reading or without reference to orality. And so on.

If rhetoric in the latter part of the nineteenth century and the early part of our own century was impoverished in the way I. A. Richards depicted it in the thirties (3–8, 23–34), contemporary rhetoric suffers from an embarrassment of riches, which can impoverish in another way—by vacuity, loss of centeredness, dilettantism. No wonder that beyond general adherence to a vague process approach (as if this were one definable notion), there is little consensus. No wonder that the vast majority of composition teachers at all levels simply ignore theory altogether. No wonder that one of our leading theorists, a person who has contributed as much as anyone to the revival of rhetoric in English departments, holds that rhetoric itself is moribund, of value only as a clearinghouse, as a place to gather and interpret the insights of the special sciences into literate processes (Winterowd). Rhetoric becomes, in this view, more or less a mediating discipline between pure scientific research on the one hand and classroom praxis on the other.

The last thing I would advocate is cessation of the dialogue, whether among ourselves or with other disciplines. That the study of writing is multidisciplinary is another one of those few propositions with which all contemporary rhetoricians can concur. At the same time, dialogics must have a center, if no more than a focus of concern. For the point of dialogue is not just exchange of knowledge and ideas but a culling of the sound from the unsound, the useful and relevant from that which is tangential, secondary, or merely, as we politely say, interesting. And we can do none of these things without knowing what we are after. Perhaps we can now seriously pose the question, What should a theory of discourse do?—not in the abstract, but concretely, for us—and turn up something better than a wish list or a set of imponderables.

For us, for practicing rhetoricians from the ancient Greeks on, our center or primary concern is getting people to speak or write more effectively than they would by aptitude and experience alone. Our task is to build on aptitude and experience by bringing to consciousness the norms of discourse types and the options for realizing these norms, so that explicit knowledge and conscious control can supplement natural ability and the tacit knowledge —the know-how—that comes from hands-on experience. Such is the art of rhetoric; on these assumptions the art stands or falls. Our center, then, is ultimately praxis and therefore social or cultural in the sense that we gauge our success by the degree to which our students perform well in those kinds of discourse our culture deems necessary or valuable, including discourse that questions traditional values and the status quo. The rhetoricians of ancient Greece taught oratory because oratory was the key to full participation in their city-states; we teach the discourse of literacy for the same reason, to enable our students to function to the limit of their capacity in a society totally dependent on writing, print, and printouts.

The very nature of our primary concern has made us students of discourse, but not in the sense in which, say, a contemporary linguist interested in pragmatics is a student of discourse. For the linguist the study of discourse is very nearly an end in itself; for us, it is finally, no matter how much we become engrossed in the study of discourse for its intrinsic fascination, a means to an end, better discoursing. The linguist strives for a theory that can explain discourse, the implicit rules that govern cohesion, for instance. Such a theory might have implications for praxis, but applications are nonessential to linguistic science per se. The rhetorician, like the linguist, wants to be able to explain how discourses work, but the application is the cake, not the icing on the cake, for rhetorical art. Finally, a linguist need not be concerned with the relative quality of the discourse under scrutiny, beyond a bare minimum of functionality; the rhetorician must make such judgments, since discovery of the best available means for realizing a discourse purpose is the business of an art of rhetoric.

My intent is not to disparage scientific assumptions, methods, or theories but rather to draw attention to the motivations that make our theories unlike those produced by our colleagues in linguistics or in any other science with a stake in discourse study. All the theories discussed in this book, with the possible exception of Moffett's, have in varying degrees scientific pretensions. But they are not really scientific and would not be taken as such by discourse science. They are actually theories of discourse meant to guide or critique rhetorical praxis, exactly what a theory of discourse should do for us. That is why they continue to engage our attention, why they are not tangential, secondary, or just "interesting." That is why they lack, by and large, the sharp focus and descriptive-analytical precision one finds routinely in scientific theory. This lack is not a defect, however, but the result of dedication to an art and the far more complex problems that confront the art of acting with language.

Multidimensionality and Dialectic

A proposition, an image, and a concept have continually recurred in my efforts to think our theories through toward a synthesis. The proposition is Britton's: "Writing cannot be regarded globally" (3). As another critic of classroom "dummy runs" puts it: no one can "write writing" (Johnson 109). We must write something, a discourse of a certain kind, for a readership, in a situation, and so forth.

If writing could be regarded globally, if, as some of our colleagues say, good writing is just good writing, rhetoric would not need a theory of discourse. We could just teach the eternal truths of good writing. However, since nothing is good or bad but the kind of discourse and situation make it so, rhetorical thought worth the name has always either assumed or formulated a theory of discourse. On this count, the major difference between Aristotle and us is that he had only to discriminate kinds of oratory, while we must cope with the far more intricate universe of written discourse.

Britton's proposition implies that rhetoric must either appropriate or produce a theory of discourse, that the two go hand in hand. Discourse theory is no luxury for the few, no mere exercise in conceptual gymnastics for those so inclined. It is essential to rhetorical thought, essential to praxis that is to any degree aware of itself. All this is obvious, I suppose, and could be passed over in silence were it not that even specialists in rhetoric fall too easily into talk about "good writing" as if it had the status of one of Plato's ideas.

The image is Moffett's "wheels within wheels," closely related to the key concept of multidimensionality, emphasized by both Moffett and Britton. Although one may not be altogether happy with a mechanistic metaphor for discourse theory, nevertheless the image that wheels within wheels conjures up is in many respects ideal: a vast clockwork of interacting parts, each essential to the functioning of the whole—turn one wheel and you turn them all, those adjacent and those far removed from the center. Composition works this way—any major change in a text causes a ripple effect, adjustments across the board. It stands to reason, therefore, that a theory of discourse responsive to the experience of composing must express somehow the complex of interacting motives in the writing process and of interrelated structures in the finished product.

Besides capturing a significant aspect of how writing feels and our intuitions about discourse processes and products, the wheels-within-wheels metaphor also helps to correct for the liabilities of exposition. I will outline a multidimensional theory, which can only take the form of a linear, each-in-turn discussion of the variables that, acting together, make discourse processes and products what they are. I can see them as a whole, but I can discuss them only one by one, abstracted and more or less isolated from each other. Furthermore, although I can suggest or point to their interworkings, I can never describe in more than a very partial way how the variables interact. The patterns are just too complex. Ultimately, then, one can express the whole only through a metaphor like wheels within wheels, the many variables mutually affecting one another being virtually impossible to convey by a set of propositions.

Talk of interaction and interworkings follows from the concept of multidimensionality, which in turn can scarcely be separated from the other key concept, dialectic, implicit also in the notion of synthesis itself. In the previous four chapters dialectic has meant dialogics, progression by critique, by a creative clash of competing formulations. Since the outcomes of that process are here assumed, dialogics has still a presence, though, so to speak, in the background. Foregrounded is the meaning of dialectic sloganized by the phrase *union of opposites*. The main opposites that must be unified are process and product. Of course, they are not really opposites, except as labels for pedagogical or critical orientations. They are really terms that mutually imply each other, any product whatsoever resulting from a process and existing as a process (i.e., in time, as dynamic, as becoming), any process whatsoever resulting in production of something. The truth, then, is that such opposites are always already unified in the sense that products imply processes and vice versa; we take them as opposites because language has us making sharp divisions or dissociations, the origin of one-sidedness.

I am not saying that teaching writing as product is the same as teaching it as a process. What I am saying is that any product theory requires a complementary theory of process; conversely, it makes no sense to teach a writing process as if process were an end in itself, as if it were not what it is, a way to an end, drafts and final or abandoned drafts. Theoretically, such a dialectical or multidimensional view means that we must be systematically inconsistent in our thinking. That is, instead of viewing a variable like aim only from the standpoint of product, as a concept for discourse classification, or only from the standpoint of process, as the purposes that we have in mind as we start to compose or discover in the act of composing, we will shift back and forth, seeing aim as both a product and process concept. We thereby forgo the virtue of consistency as it is usually understood in theoretical evaluation, but we overcome the one-sidedness of theories praised for rigorous adherence to a single perspective.

The Variables

I have grouped the nine variables into three categories: the act variables: aim and genre, subject matter and mode, media, and context; the agent variables: writer and reader, editor and teacher; and the process variables: the composing process proper, which begins with the urge or necessity to write, and the precomposing process, which takes into account inquiry of all sorts, discourse acts not connected directly to any act of written composition. I make no theoretical claim for the division into act, agent, and process variables. Sheer expository convenience is my only motive. I do, however, claim exhaustiveness for the variables themselves: we need nothing else to account for any discourse.

I can detect no reason to arrange the variables in any hierarchical relationship. Simply by the foci of their discussions, our four theorists imply that some of these variables are more important than others. Kinneavy explicitly argues for aim as the prime variable. Walter H. Beale's theory advances not only a hierarchy of concepts but also categories that interlock, the end of the "higher" category being also the beginning of the next "lower" one (16). Such strongly vertical modes of organization ignore too much the horizontal dimension, the protean unpredictability of discourse as it is experienced.

All theories must idealize, of course. The question is one of degree: how much awareness of horizontal complexity one is willing to sacrifice for vertical integration, a central tension in all systematic thought. This push-pull cannot be escaped, but it can be handled in markedly different ways. I see that any discourse or discourse process will, on analysis, evince a hierarchy of relations among the variables. But what this hierarchy is cannot be settled in advance. A relatively straightforward example is the variable of editor-teacher. Much writing, especially when not intended for publication, lacks this factor altogether in its motivational mix, while many works in any library only exist because some editor made a discourse out of somebody's lecture notes or personal papers. Such an editor's motives will often be of high importance in explaining the discourse. To take a more complicated example: it would seem that discourse mode will a priori always be subordinate to discourse aim or genre. So Kinneavy holds, and one must agree insofar as one normally, for example, tells a story in order to accomplish some end—to inform, persuade, entertain. Even here, however, where a hierarchy would seem almost compelled by logic, we know from experience that means are always becoming ends in themselves, taking on an independent validity or value beyond function or even contrary to function. Much academic German philosophy is notorious for a jargon-ridden complexity far beyond the needs of technical or argumentative precision. Indeed, at times the fog becomes so dense that one can make nothing out. Such obscurity for its own sake is really a sign of belonging, like a secret society's password or ritual handshake; consciously cultivated at first, it becomes habitual in exactly the same way that a bureaucrat, who has learned to obfuscate for self-protection, obfuscates even when nothing is at stake. Thus, means become ends, even to the impairment or total loss of intelligibility.

In contrast, then, to much discourse theory, I have resisted the urge to rank the variables. What matters is to have a vocabulary developed sufficiently to cope with discourse, to explain it and to teach it. Moreover, how the variables interact is far more important for concrete understanding than their rank ordering, even if all discourse manifested the same motives in the same proportions, making a universal hierarchy possible. It is best, I think, not to try to decree hierarchy in advance but to let it emerge according to the particulars of each case.

CHAPTER SIX

THE ACT VARIABLES

Aim and Genre

At the beginning of Chapter 5, I noted that much of what had been said in the previous four chapters had now to be assumed. This is especially so with the aim concept and its implications, discussed at considerable length in the chapters devoted to Kinneavy and Britton. The conclusions reached there furnish our point of departure here.

Although aim is not absolutely more important than the other variables, it has a historical, practical, and systematic centrality that none of the others can claim. As Kinneavy points out, the liberal arts tradition, with its roots in classical education, attempts to educate people in various uses or aims of language, rhetoric being originally one of them, the art of oratory. Beyond even this historical connection of aim with rhetoric, aim is practically or pedagogically indispensable to the overall sense of a writing task and is a major factor in sustaining concentration and energy for completing the task. Finally, aim also has a systematic or theoretical significance in that discriminations by aim structure much discourse theory from Aristotle on; the theories of Kinneavy and Britton are but two of many organized by the aim variable.

If one adds to this what seems a reasonable position—that discourse typologies should lead directly to rhetorical arts for each type—one can see why I have expended so much effort trying to pin down the concept itself as well as the best typology that can emerge from the quite different approaches of Kinneavy and Britton.

The following assertions summarize my view of the aim concept itself:

1. Aim is a judgment based on the recognition of convention and justified by reasoning. It is not, therefore, objective—there, in a text—but an interpre-

tation, really intersubjective in that discourse conventions exist only as the tacit or explicit norms of a language community. Consequently, one cannot verify an aim judgment simply by appeal to textual features. Rather, one must argue, advancing good reasons for any disputed interpretation of aim, reasons backed both by textual "point-at-ables" and by extratextual knowledge. In the final analysis, then, a judgment or an interpretation of aim amounts to a persuasive act; it says, in effect, See the text this way, as designed to achieve this purpose, and you will understand it better.

2. Consequently, aim does not constitute a class concept in the same sense that, for example, homo sapiens does. Homo sapiens isolates a species that can be differentiated sharply from other human species by concrete, measurable features; aim is either an inductive leap to motive based on conventions a text observes and knowledge of the circumstances of composition, or it is a writer's statement of intent, self-interpretation. In both cases aim is heuristic, an act of disclosure about the "unseen" domain of motive, not a designation for a demarcated species of existents to which certain individuals clearly belong.

Let me elaborate a bit on the systematic implications of my second assertion. Judgments about aim tend always to be problematical, uncertain. Differences of opinion are bound to arise, whether the hermeneutic focus is a finished text or the judgment of a writer, reader, or mentor about a draft or a partial draft. Usually, however, we can reach a consensus about aims or at least comprehend exactly why our interpretations diverge. The real problem with aim arises when we try to convert it from persuasive-heuristic status to a class concept, as both Kinneavy and Britton try to do in correlating discourse features and strategies directly with the aims and functions their respective models generate. Such a move ineluctably encounters the stubborn fact of asymmetry—that discourse motives correlate very unreliably with so-called typical patterns of logic, organization, or style (Beale 19). Take the persuasive aim, for instance. Perhaps we think spontaneously of case structure as a norm for this type: a central contention supported by reasons in turn supported by evidence of some sort. But it is just as normal or typical to persuade without a single enthymeme; much persuasion takes the form of a narrative or story, as in the parables attributed to Jesus in the Bible. And in certain circumstances merely a recitation of data without explicit conclusions can be powerfully persuasive.

How can we escape this trap? On the one hand, it is hard to see how rhetoric could dispense with aim or, without denying its own history, ignore aim's systematic significance. An aim typology of some sort seems essential. On the other hand, the aims of discourse cannot be directly associated with discourse surfaces—features, forms, means, tactics—whatever labels one attaches to "observables" in discourses; an aim typology may adequately discriminate possible motives for writing, but it cannot discriminate discourse classes.

In the Kinneavy chapter, I offered a possible solution to this problem: localize aim; consider it always in relation to discourse in a definite time and place, and aim can become a generic as well as a heuristic notion. In this way we can recognize the scientific motive at work in a vast array of discourses from cultures and historical periods even totally unconnected with one another, while confining scientific discourse to something more manageable, more describable, such as what Kuhn calls modern "normal" science. We can, in other words, avoid ethnocentricity by granting what is indisputably true: that the conventions of scientific writing vary enormously from place to place and time to time and yet concentrate on our kind of scientific discourse, the conventions of which we must be able to articulate for our students if we intend to teach scientific writing.

Localizing aim solves our problem—almost. We still have to avoid merely arbitrary choices of focus. For example, though Kinneavy recognizes a range of exploratory writing, what he really means by exploration—how he localizes it—is somewhat arbitrary in that his attention is almost exclusively on scientific exploration. The process of discovering and articulating hypotheses for scientific research is surely one of the more culturally significant genres of written exploration, but no more significant than theoretical dialogics in literary criticism, philosophy of science, rhetoric, and so forth. And the panel discussion has become perhaps the commonest type of exploratory discourse, encountered daily on news programs and other public forums.

To make a precise and fully self-conscious move from the motive-heuristic concept of aim to the generic concept of localized aim requires another term, *genre*—or better, what Beale designates "de facto genre" (24). Basically, the notion of de facto genre recognizes that no theory of discourse can derive or deduce actual uses of language in the same way that Kinneavy and Britton generated the aims and functions from the communication triangle. Genres belong to history, arising in response to social and cultural factors peculiar to a time and place. They are in no sense a priori: one can extract the persuasive aim from the implications of foregrounding the decoder in Kinneavy's model, but one cannot deduce Aristotle's genres of oratory or Augustine's rhetoric of the sermon. The logic of a genre's existence derives from sociocultural givens like a legal system, a democratic debate of public policy, the heeding of the Macedonian call, or the need to manage somehow vast quantities of data, as in the contemporary technical reports of our governmental agencies and businesses.

At this point, someone might plausibly ask, Why deal with aim at all?

Why not simply develop rhetorics for the de facto genres we intend to teach? After all, to deal with convention at any relatively concrete level requires thinking about genres, not aims. Can't we, by Occam's principle, dispense with aim altogether?

In retaining aim, we are not multiplying concepts beyond necessity. Most obviously, judgments about aim will still have to be made, since genres may have multiple aims, some writing will be difficult or impossible to classify by genre, and some writing will appropriate the conventions of one genre for use in another. We also require aim for the systematic demands of theory. De facto genres are in a sense ad hoc: they are just there; they happen to exist as the conventions or categorical expectations of the business letter, the newspaper editorial, the sonnet, and so on. As such, they have the advantage of being more concrete than aim. But they have also the disadvantage of being asystematic in two senses: they cannot be deduced from the structure of the discourse act itself, as aim can, and with respect to each other they bear no intrinsic relations (genres per se can only be inventoried; the aims imply one another and are self-generated from the communication triangle). Put another way; we cannot organize genres except in relation to the "higher" concept of aim. We do this spontaneously when we group together as types of literature the short story, the novel, the lyric poem, the epic, and so on. What we are actually doing is relating de facto genres to a shared motive, the literary aim.

Finally, we *must* organize genres with aims, not only because without the aim concept we can have only a random list of genres but also because most (but not all) instances of genres with a common aim will evince some shared features or tactics. Aristotle recognized the differences between aim and genre by distinguishing kinds of oratory (Cooper 16–17). In like manner, we need to distinguish norms belonging to each of the aims as well as the more specific conventions that guide discourse in all genres classifiable within an aim.

It is essential that we be completely clear about the theoretical move just made regarding aim and genre, especially the localizing of aim. The association of aim with genre is at least as old as Aristotle. Kinneavy and Britton both give generic instances of their aims and individual discourses exemplifying genres and aims. What I am proposing, then, is scarcely a departure from tradition; I too want to organize the universe of discourse by grouping genres by predominant aim. Moreover, and this next suggestion is traditional as well, I think we should develop rhetorics for all written genres, or if that is too ambitious, at least for those genres we intend to teach. Just as Augustine developed a rhetorical art of the sermon, a persuasive genre that did not exist in Aristotle's Athens, so we have the task of isolating the norms and strategies of written discourse. One way to go about this mam-

moth task is to discriminate so far as possible aim-specific norms and strategies from genre-specific ones. We can then teach (bring to a fuller conscious
awareness) both the norms that belong to an aim and the norms that belong
to genres *within* an aim. For example, there are the general needs and
problems of informing, and there are the specific conventions of, say, the
encyclopedia article and the technical report.

In pursuing these ends—and here is my contribution to the argument,
with an assist from Beale—we must not confuse the aim concept with the
genre concept. Perhaps it is natural to use the terms interchangeably, to
impute to aim the presence or status of genre. Aims are judgments or
inferences about motive, often arguable, made during and after the fact of
composition; genres are quasi-objective discourse types generally recognized by a language community or some group within that community.
Although aims and genres are both recognized through conventions, aims
are heuristic in both interpretation and in their sorting out of the de facto
genres that happen to exist in some culture at some time, while genres are
a genuine class concept, designating a species of discourse by recurrent
features.

With aim alone we are doomed to excessively leaky categories. If we can
hold fast to the aim-genre distinction, the problem of asymmetry becomes
manageable; we also stand a better chance of avoiding explicit or implicit
reduction of aim to a single genre. The presence of both terms pushes us
to develop rhetorics that distinguish as much as possible between what one
finds in all or most instances of the expressive aim and what is peculiar to
genres that share the aim—the diary, the spontaneous testimonial, the manifesto. In this way, our advice to students can be much more specific and
concrete than it would be by relying on aim alone.

Of course, the genre concept itself is problematical. Genre classifications
leak too. Differences of opinion will arise over both the features of genres
and whether or not discourse *x* belongs to genre *y*. Nevertheless, genre is
necessary because we cannot teach "writing" any more than we can write
"writing"; we can only teach and write kinds of writing. Aim is too abstract
and not really a generic concept anyway—hence, the necessity of genre to
deal with kind more concretely.

To those who would condemn any division of discourse as a fiction or
falsification, as the imposition of static categories on the dynamic, protean
domain of language use, I can only say, yes, they do falsify, but they "lie"
in a creative or productive way indispensable to praxis; and yes, they are
static where discourse is always in process, but this means only that aims
and genres must also be viewed dynamically as well as statically in the total
dialectic of these two concepts. In short, the critics are right: theories always
fictionalize and falsify. But as long as we understand what we are doing

and do it with the right attitude, without becoming self-convinced or rigid, we stand to gain part of the necessary fictions without which no art or field of study can function.

Turning now from the aim concept to a model of aims, I offer for consideration figure 1.

Let me comment briefly on the rationale and implications of this graphic. First, note the retention of the communication triangle itself. It has been attacked as a schema best suited to oral discourse (Hunter 286). Without explaining why, Beale also rejects the triangle as a model for his own theory of written discourse (59). Apparently there is some agreement that the triangle is less than ideal for handling written discourse.

Nevertheless, I have retained it for two reasons. It is implicit in all four of our theories, prominent in three. No synthesis, therefore, could discard the triangle without good reason, which I have yet to find. Theory must work from some foundation, some irreducible minimum notions. The triangle constitutes one set of irreducible notions: there really are languages

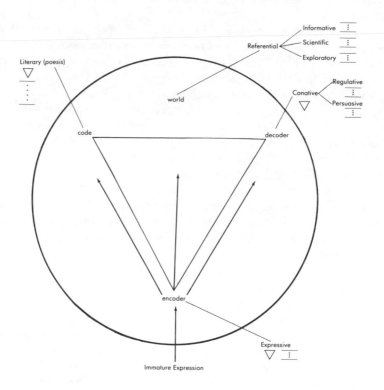

Figure 1.

(codes), speakers and writers (encoders), audiences and readerships (decoders); take away any one of the three, and discourse cannot exist. These three defining components of the discourse act, these sine qua nons, constitute the irreducible minimum of thought about discourse. They also have, necessarily, an archaic or primitive presence: from the first discourse act, they must be implicitly there. No wonder, then, that Kinneavy finds the triangle in a host of discourse theorists extending back to Aristotle: analyze any discourse act—oral, written, printed, electronically processed—and you will find some version of the triangular relations.

Of course, the media variable does matter a great deal. It will receive attention shortly. For now, however, the point is that our basic aim model is still an extrapolation from the communication triangle, despite—or, rather, because—the triangle itself originated from an analysis of speech acts. Its oral bias is an asset, not a liability, since all language use is grounded directly or indirectly in speech.

Note also the substitution of *world* for *reality* in Kinneavy's model and the encompassing of the triangle by the circle of *world*. The commonsense notion of *reality* as that which exists "out there" probably functions well enough for general purposes. In any case, we all spontaneously use reality in the sense of the objective world. Moreover, an important aim of discourse is supposed to "say it like it is," depict reality without bias or the intrusion of personal visions. From the standpoint of convention, it does not matter that no human being can actually be objective, nor does it matter that we never have reality but that we only have some intersubjective construct of it.

Theoretically, however, it does matter. "World" is always what human beings actually have, a mostly tacit construct of what has been, is, and will be, a complex of images, metaphors, guiding assumptions, "facts," prejudices, and so forth. This world, in actuality a horizon of meanings that makes experience possible and alters in response to experience, is the reality that preoccupies the referential aim (Gadamer, *Truth* 269, 402, 405); hence the designation *world* in our model and the linking of the referential motive with it.

The communication triangle is placed within the world circle because any discourse act presupposes world and transpires within it. The place of world is not captured well by making it, like Kinneavy's reality, a mere point on the triangle. This designation levels world, as if world had the same status as code, decoder, and encoder, as if it were just one of four essentials for discoursing. World, however, does and does not belong to discourse. It is prior to language use in the sense that world is what discourse reveals; in this sense, it is the given, and discourse only brings parts of it to presence. But world is also what language *makes*, since a reality construct can hardly be constructed without language. Resulting from the interaction of the given and the made, world clearly is not just an element or a component of discourse; rather it is the milieu of discourse, the total view of things implicit in a language, a culture, the scene that contains the act, in Kenneth Burke's terminology (*Grammar* 3).

The aims are depicted as they are to emphasize their nature as high-level abstractions. As an interpretative system extrapolated from the triangle (itself an abstraction, of course), the aim concept belongs to world in that all human interpretation must arise within the world it would illuminate. In this sense, the aims should also be, like the triangle itself, depicted within the world's circle. I have placed the aims outside as a constant reminder of their abstract nature and also, incidentally, to achieve better visual separation for the graphic itself.

The vertical dotted line bounded on either side by short horizontal lines under each aim represents the genres, a finite but unspecifiable list that can only be filled out with each localization of the aim model—each application to a particular time and place.

The small triangle under each aim is my way of recognizing the factor of continuum without resorting to a maze of lines linking each of the aims to all the other aims. If, as part of an interpretation of discourse *x*, we assign it to a predominating aim (if possible, to a genre within that aim), we may apply the triangle again to assess the relative mix of the other aims, all being to some degree present in any discourse complicated enough to demand extensive interpretation. In this way, we provide systematically for the discourse that is poetic-cum-persuasive ("A Modest Proposal"), poetic-cum-expressive ("Tintern Abbey"), and poetic-cum-referential (*A Journal of the Plague Year*).

Finally, note the inclusion of Britton's category *immature expression*. It is not an aim, of course, since by definition it is the undifferentiated matrix out of which the aims develop. As a term designating the all-purpose discourse of young children, it may also be thought of as pretriangular, since children must learn the code and decenter enough to conceive a decoder distinct from a self in order for the discourse relationships depicted by the triangle to emerge fully.

The mapping of immature expression onto the encoder is meant to recall Britton's hypothesis that the expressive aim comes first, not necessarily in the sense of actual first or early utterances but in the sense that the most congenial route to the world of adult discourse runs through expression. The other aims presumably develop by suppression or subordination of the expressive aim to achieve one or several of the others, a gradual process depicted here by arrows emanating from the encoder in the direction of code, world, and decoder.

★ ★ ★

So much, then, for the aim and genre concepts, the relation between them, and the general model of the aims.

The general title of the second part of this study is "A Dialogical Synthesis—and Beyond." A synthesis, if it is worth anything, must carry us beyond what is synthesized, and I have moved past our four theories as well by bringing Beale's thought on asymmetry and the aim-genre relation into the picture. But beyond this beyond is an indefinite list of questions for which I have no answer. For example, does expressive discourse really come first? Or is it rather that narrative comes first, fictive, nonfictive, semifictive, children perhaps in a small way recapitulating our preliterate ancestors and their epic cycles? If expression can be taught most easily, what forms does it take? What are the first instances of the other aims like? What are the intermediate forms for all the aims? What should we teach to help move a student from some form of immature persuasion to a more mature form? And so on.

Or take another list of related questions. Given that aim and genre are only concepts for breaking down the churning lump of discourse, for seeing something besides an undifferentiated mass, do aims possess any psychological reality? Do people innocent of modern rhetorical theory differentiate discourse motives in some way to some degree as a rhetorician consciously employing our theory would? When does genre awareness emerge? Why and how? Furthermore, people clearly do not get their purposes for writing from contemplating the triangle or fall so in love with a particular genre that they write just to produce something in it. How, then, do the living purposes of people composing connect with aims and genres?

I raise these questions because they are interesting, important, and answerable, and also to indicate how modest our advance has been. Even if this synthesis should receive a degree of tentative acceptance, it raises a host of questions that will take us far beyond its effective guidance.

Finally, we need to remember that aim is not just a model-making concept but also vital in the act of composing itself. D'Angelo held that purpose is part of the initiating gestalt of composing, the sense of the whole within which actual drafting occurs. Purpose may just as well arise during composing, but in any case where does it come from? Clearly it comes from exigence, which must be understood as arising not from needs or demands that are just there but from an interpretation of what is appropriate. Probably most of the time conventional expectation is so obvious in exigence that we are quite unaware of interpretation at all. A committee has finished its deliberations, reached a consensus. The next step is to satisfy exigence, to issue a report of its findings to whatever authority or constituency established the committee in the first place. We know that the report must be informative (perhaps cum persuasive) and that it must conform to one of the genres such a report always takes, for example, the interoffice memo. In such routine, sheerly functional contexts, we are working with ossified interpretations, conventions so imperious that they feel objectively there.

The interpretative role of aim in the composing process is clearer in cases where exigence arises more from within than from without. In the example sketched above, it would be fatuous to ask, What am I trying to do? Everyone knows what must be done. In self-driven writing, however, the aim question is seldom fatuous. Workable self-interpretations can indeed be enabling, the difference that makes all the difference. For example, four years ago when I first started this project, I experienced a profound uneasiness that brought all work to a halt. I had to change my concept of aim. I had thought of theory as basically persuasive, the advancing of good reasons for holding a particular viewpoint. But *a* viewpoint was exactly wrong for this project, which had about it disquieting oedipal overtones anyway, since the theorists had been my teachers through their books and one had been a kind of senior guru; they were thus ideal to double as father figures. Slowly my aim changed from persuasive to exploratory, altering stance and tone accordingly. Meanwhile, Hegel had shown me how to operate with a dialectical many-sidedness without a loss of critical sharpness (and, incidentally, without "father-kill" either, Hegel's evolutionary view admitting no such simplistic joys). At this point my problem was solved, my uneasiness dissolved, and progress could be made with no more than the usual difficulties of putting any book together.

Aim is not, then, only an abstraction suitable for making discourse typologies. It is concretely at work in the process of composing, especially as part of a writer's self-understanding.

Subject Matter and Mode

Clearly subject matter and mode are significant and closely related variables. It is by no means clear, however, how to handle them for our purposes. In the final analysis subject matter and mode are beyond anyone's competence. No English teacher, regardless of intelligence and extent of education, can know intimately the demands of these variables in all the divisions and subdivisions of English, much less in any other field. In the absence of genuine writing across the curriculum, without circumstances permitting and teachers willing to allot the time and effort to student apprenticeship, subject matter and mode cannot really be handled at all.

Granting, then, that we can know neither the various subject matters nor the sometimes esoteric logics, mathematical operations, canons of proof, and so on, that constitute their means, nevertheless a general theory of discourse needs some overall view of both variables. Among our four theorists, the best conception is Moffett's.

There is mind. There is the world, thought of as external to mind. And there is language, mind-making, the great mediator. There is no immediate approach to either mind or world, only the mediate way of language. We can, however, discern relative degrees of abstraction in both subject-matter areas and modes of discourse. History is more concrete, closer to the structure of world, while logic and math are closer to the structure of mind. Within fields we can detect also the continuum between world and mind: Bloomfield-style structural linguistics, for example, with its predilection for field studies of actual languages, was closer to the thing itself than, say, the Chomsky-inspired search for a universal grammar.

One reason that some fields or ways of inquiry within fields are or seem more concrete than others has to do with dominant mode of discourse. Closest to the temporal structure of experience is the chronological mode —conventional histories, reports of what happened, based in part on first-hand accounts. More abstract is the analogic mode, which groups objects or events into classes based on the detection of likenesses and generalizes about the class as a whole. The difference between a history and a theory of history—Marx's, for example—is in part a difference of mode, chronologic versus analogic. Finally, there is language used to talk about language, tautologic, as, for example, in a philosophy of history that concerns itself with the field's central concepts. Thus, we have a modal continuum, defined at one end by on-the-scene reporting, relatively close to world, and at the other end by discourse that uses language to examine language, in its concern with the mind's categories per se, presumably close to the structure of mind.

Such in a nutshell is Moffett's view of subject matter and mode implicit in his discussion of the I-it relation. His notion of mode parallels Kinneavy's in large part, chronologic taking in the latter's narration and description, analogic being the same as classification, while Kinneavy's evaluation amounts essentially to a judgment of merit among classes of objects, performances, and so on, thus being dependent on the analogic mode. (To say that movie x is better than movie y obviously presupposes classification as movies. Hence, we can treat evaluation as an extension or implication of analogic.)

We need, then, lose nothing from Kinneavy's modal system in adopting Moffett's. And we gain much more than just an additional, significant category, tautologic, the dominant mode, for example, of dialectic and treatises on logic and math, to name only a few of many instances of discourses that amount to words about words or symbolizing about symbols. Most important, what we gain is something better than a mere list of modes, whether short like Kinneavy's or long as in the textbook tradition of means of development (e.g., narration, description, comparison and contrast, argument). For Moffett's modes build progressively on each other, an account of what happened often drawing on eyewitness testimony, while generalizing or theorizing about what happens involves reflection on many instances of what happened, and tautologic in turn depends on theory, being often a critique of theory itself, a dialectical examination of arguments. Furthermore, in moving by degrees from the relatively less abstract (the selectivity of perception in on-the-scene accounts of what is happening) to the relatively more abstract (the selectivity of memory in reports on what happened, of genre or class thinking in analogic, and finally of discourse about class concepts themselves), Moffett's modes discriminate levels of intellectual operations in or behind all discourse and discourse processes as well as approximating stages in the intellectual development of students.

No other modal theory I know of, including the quite different approach advanced by Beale (36–48), can claim the advantages of Moffett's, especially the pedagogical advantages. The key is the interconnectedness of Moffett's categories, which work against conceiving the modes only as options for the writer or as a scheme of analysis for finished discourses. Rather, because of the movement built into Moffett's understanding of the modes, anyone working with his view will naturally incline to see the dynamic interaction of the modes rather than their mere presence. One can begin, for example, to see more clearly how certain writing assignments require students to pass back and forth between two or more levels of abstraction. One can then consciously design assignment sequences better, so that later writing tasks draw on intellectual abilities developed in earlier ones. More than this, we can help students become aware of the implications of their own processes. It is not enough that they are able to report what is happening; they must also discover why they saw one thing rather than another, what their principles of perceptual selection are. It is not enough that they can work with abstract concepts; they must discover what difference it makes to confront the "same experience" with a different set of concepts, a different way of seeing. This is what Moffett means by teaching students to play the whole symbolic scale and to know where they are on it at any given time. A process approach, then, certainly, but optimally a process that understands itself. That is the goal that informs Moffett's view of the I-it relation.

Let me summarize. Though not presented as such, Moffett's exploration of the I-it relation amounts to a modal theory. It is also a schema of subject areas (if not specifically of subject matters) that allows us to estimate where a particular field belongs with respect to other fields on the scale of abstraction, helping us in turn to explore with our students how, for example, philosophy differs from science or how a theory of history differs from history itself. As a modal theory Moffett's I-it relation is the best we have. It has a rationale of high generality: the continuum between world and mind. It is capable of embracing other modal theories, such as Kinneavy's. And Moffett's modes, unlike all others I am aware of, are genuinely dynamic, interconnected, interacting, not merely a set of static categories artificially separated from each other as so many means of development. Moffett's approach is genuinely a process approach to modality, one with immediate and manifold applications for composition pedagogy.

In advocating Moffett's approach as our most promising modal theory, I feel that certain limitations must be stressed. As with any theoretical concept, of course, Moffett's modes are only as good as the teacher using them. Applied inflexibly and without imagination, they might even prove deleterious; for example, in the hands of a teacher who sees them in a lockstep, linear fashion, Moffett's rich understanding of their interaction could degenerate into a singleminded drive toward ever greater abstraction, as if abstraction were an absolute good.

Despite this permanent limitation on all theories of anything in our field, we need to develop Moffett's categories themselves and work with them in relation to the other discourse variables, especially aim and genre. Whether as Britton develops it or otherwise, clearly we need a more detailed view of analogic than Moffett offers, one that discriminates stages of growth from a child's first comparisons to sophisticated, adult-level manipulation of concepts. We also require a more explicit understanding of how the developing analogic mode affects perception and memory (the basis of selection in the lower modes). Finally, we must not reduce the modes, as Moffett does, to information processing. In persuasion, for example, often the key move is a substitution of one concept for another or a dissociation of concepts that unreflective use associates. Here is analogic at work, but the method and the ends differ from those one would find in, say, an encyclopedia article. The modes work differently—they have distinctive kinds of presence and force—in the various aims and genres; this, too, demands our attention, if we are to progress beyond a superficial grasp of modality.

Media

While all our theories recognize the media variable to some degree, none of them advances a comprehensive view or explores any part of such a view to any great depth. Perhaps this seems surprising, since celebrated publications by scholars such as McLuhan, Havelock, and Ong preceded our theories by at least five years and helped to create a new level of interest in media, especially the electronic world of the "global village" (Havelock, *Muse* 24–29). But it is really not so surprising that our theories have relatively little to say in this area. Intense interest in questions of orality and literacy in our field has emerged only recently, after the usual lag time between scholarly innovation and general acceptance. Furthermore, there was not the standing, traditional concern with media in rhetoric and composition with which to assimilate the new knowledge, or any obvious way to comprehend the extraordinarily complex media variable. Even now, when all composition professionals can intelligently discuss the differing demands of speaking and writing, we still have no comprehensive, systematic media theory, in part because no single person can command knowledge of a subject that spans a number of disciplines and many intensely studied areas of specialization. It would be difficult, for example, to keep up with research in even a single medium, such as television or film, impossible to know more than a small fraction of the total work going on.

Granting this limitation of knowledge, which applies as well to all the discourse variables (consider, for example, the vast literature on the single mode of narration in *poesis* or on the genres of legal rhetoric), the study of media has nevertheless progressed far enough to bring our task into view. A general theory of discourse must comprehend Ong's phases in the transmission of the word: primary orality (preliteracy), writing, print, and secondary orality (the electronic media) (*Presence* 22–92). *Comprehend* here means or includes at minimum the following: understanding each phase after primary orality as simultaneously dependent on its predecessor and independent of its predecessor in bringing new conditions for discourse into existence; seeing these new conditions (which have both social and psychological dimensions) concretely in terms of the other variables; and, most important, striving to uncover the interaction of the verbal technologies in past and present discourse.

A comprehensive media theory must be developed not only because a general theory of discourse is incomplete without it but also because no aspect of language teaching can now ignore the factor of media. In literary studies, the evidence is overwhelming that the Homeric epic cannot be understood apart from the culture of primary orality (Ong, *Orality* 17–27), nor can we explain how *Paradise Lost* differs from its ancient heritage without a grasp of how high literacy differs from pre- or nonliteracy. In linguistics the awareness has been developing for some time that the analysis of conversation and the analysis of written discourse require distinctive pragmatic approaches: that the norms or rules of the one are not the norms or rules of the other. And in rhetoric and composition, our task is almost defined by the media: assist in the delivery of literate minds out of the womb of preliteracy, where all human beings begin and where many remain as semi-

or nonliterates. For learning to write amounts to more than mere mastery of a more elaborate code than speech; it means becoming literate in the full cultural sense of the phrase, the making of reading and writing into second nature, deeply internalized as a total way of thinking and acting.

So far as writing instruction is concerned, what matters most in a general theory of media is the transition in our students from preliteracy to literacy and the continuing impact of orality on literacy and vice versa—none of which, it is fair to say, we understand very well at present. Theoretically, what matters most is determining the place or role that the oral-literate distinction ought to play in our guiding theory of discourse.

Light on the developmental-pedagogical dimension comes mainly from Moffett and Britton; the issue of media's theoretical role is raised implicitly by Kinneavy's hierarchical view of the field of English, where arts and media are treated as one of three major divisions of pragmatics (*Theory* 31). I attempt to merge the former's dynamic view with the latter's static one, while advancing the argument a step or two beyond where they left it by bringing in more recently published materials.

If our concern with media were purely typological or explanatory in the sense of accounting for discourse products, Kinneavy's approach to media would probably suffice; though Kinneavy did comparatively little with the media variable, his theory would allow us to distinguish among, say, a persuasive speech, a persuasive dialogue, and written persuasion. If we need other categories to handle, for example, electronic advertising, these could be added to his categories without altering his theory in any fundamental way.

Clearly our theory must be able to account for the differences between Martin Luther King's "I Have a Dream" speech and his written apologia "Letter from Birmingham Jail." The persuasive tactics of the two pieces differ considerably, and part of the difference is oral versus written (printed) media. Supposing, however, that we could understand how the aim-genre variable interacts with the media variable, we have done nothing with the process side of media at all. We cannot even claim to handle aim and genre adequately so long as we have aim and media in two different places, artificially abstracted from each other, as if we could generate categories by mechanically matching our list of aims and genres with our list of media. For, as Ong shows very clearly, some kinds of discourse owe their existence to writing and print (*Orality* 27–28, 105–08, 127–28, 134–35). Without writing, for example, there can be no formal logic; without formal logic, nothing that we would recognize as scientific or philosophical discourse. Hence, pairing aims or genres with media would generate categories that do not in fact exist: oral scientific discourse, for example, is a class with no members. The cultures of primary orality do not produce scientific discourse

in our sense (which is not to say that they do not study the world around
them in minute ways that appear scientific and probably are protoscientific).
In our own culture scientific discourse (as distinct from the shoptalk of
scientists) may be presented orally, but it is not really oral; it is always
heavily dependent on published sources, almost always a reading and not
a speaking, and typically in need of a most unoral device, visual aids.
Scientific discourse, then, is literate, both historically in origin and developmentally in education, and no students are genuinely ready for scientific
writing until they are well along the path to literacy.

It is in contemplating this path to literacy (a phrase too linear, too singular,
and too trite to express what is going on) that we uncover the liabilities of
the typological theory, the method of analyze and separate. It is here especially that we must counter the static, conceptual theory with its dialectical, interactive counterpart if we are to have any hope at all of concretely
grasping orality and literacy as a process.

The chief barrier is our own highly developed sense of the contrast between orality and literacy. Ong's *Orality and Literacy* discusses nine ways
that the culture and discourse of primary orality differ from writing and
print (36–57). Almost any informed rhetorician could produce at least as
long a list of the contrasting features of, say, conversation as opposed to
an essay. The contrasts are certainly implicit, and they light up whole areas
of thought—from how Homer created to what students must assimilate to
compose in writing. But they also tend to throw into darkness the central
fact about becoming literate: that, from our first struggles to match signs
with sounds, *the spoken and the written are never really separated.* Rather, sounds
are the base of signs, and optimally the two become tightly interwoven,
the mature writer striving for such oral values as the right voice or tone,
the literate speaker approaching, especially on formal occasions, the syntax
and diction of writing.

But if the written and the spoken become tightly interwoven, they do
not begin that way. Doubtless Moffett is correct in holding that the ability
to write depends on "soloing out of ensembles," holding forth alone without
the prompting of conversational interlocutors. Not only are first writings
dependent on oral monologues; they tend, as Britton says, to be little more
than speech written down. Students on the threshold of literacy do not
differentiate speech and writing at all—or, if they do, not in a way that
affects behavior. Mainly by exposure, by reading, they acquire the graph-
olect and gradually internalize its special demands, such as fictionalizing a
readership and creating a context within the text. They develop toward
knowing differences between writing and speech, toward the status of many
of our better college freshman, able to turn out on demand "correct" and
functional but lifeless and voiceless prose. The last or mature phase, then,

is integration: they must preserve what they have learned about the written medium, and they must recapture certain oral values lost by too rigidly separating talk from writing (Kroll 36–41).

Even in the middle phase, however, the oral and the written are still intimately connected. All writing necessarily moves from articulate thought, inner speech, to the more elaborated code of the written language. Thought itself, therefore, is oral in origin and has its life in inner dialogue, the mind's posing and counterposing to itself. Moreover, before, during, and after the composing process, writing promotes and is nurtured by dialogue, by conversations with meaningful others about a preliminary idea, a draft, a final text. Finally, while fluent, mature reading bypasses oral mediation, processing directly from visual cues to meaning, many writers subvocalize, saying and hearing all or part of the next sentence they are about to write, however much this saying and hearing may be altered in the struggle to inscribe.

To summarize: contrasting the oral and the written helps us to formulate what students must learn in order to become writers as well as talkers; but integrating the two, appreciating and promoting their interaction, is mainly what we need in the actual teaching. The emphasis both Britton and Moffett place on the cultivation of oral interaction is anything but an overemphasis. We know that students must read to become writers; we tend to forget, in our pathologically fragmented curriculums (English is here, speech there), that written fluency depends on oral fluency. At bottom, it comes to this: if we do not listen and respond to what our students have to say, they have no reason to suffer the pain of writing. For ultimately, writing, despite its differences from speech, is irreducibly a saying, with all the nakedness, the hazards and rewards, that always attend self-assertion.

If dissociating orality and literacy conceals underlying processes, pondering this relation as if it had no interplay with other discourse variables also falsifies. It is especially important to see general intellectual growth in the context of becoming literate. Commonly one hears discussion of the transition from concrete to formal operations as if it were as natural and inevitable as a normal child's acquisition of speech. But the capacity for abstract thought, especially for the conscious conceptual analysis and manipulation so necessary for certain kinds of writing, does not develop, as Vygotsky insisted over fifty years ago, in the absence of social reinforcement (51). Part of this reinforcement is literacy itself. One might even argue that much of the kind of thought summed up in the term *formal operations* really amounts to literate thinking. For neither nonliterate cultures nor preliterate children operate with concepts the way we do, and neither can see much point in conceptual analysis. Reading and writing may very well be the single most important factor in intellectual development, especially in its upper reaches. Rather than say what pushes what, however, I would only insist that our idea of cognitive development contains a largely unrecognized literate standard and that cognition and literacy must interact in complex ways that require detailed investigation.

We cannot pursue here the many crisscrossing routes of interrelation between media and other discourse variables. Because of the prominence accorded aim in most discourse theories, including this one, it may be useful to reflect a bit more on how becoming literate impacts the discourse aims.

The model of the aims advanced in this chapter depicts two conclusions reached elsewhere in this study: that we ought not to privilege any aim of discourse in our notion of ideal, adult-level competence; that the center of gravity in preliteracy and the earlier stages of literacy is expressive discourse. I would still affirm both conclusions. Hence, I have derived the mature aims, as Kinneavy does, from the neutral ground of the communication triangle while incorporating Britton's emphasis on the developmental priority of expression.

In concentrating on ideal, adult-level competence, our model implies nothing about what actually happens to the aims as we move from preliteracy to mature literacy. What I think does happen is a gradual shift in the center of gravity from expression to persuasion. In the world of adult writing, relatively pure instances of expression are rare, apart from writing intended for the author's eyes only—diaries, journals, and the like. Perhaps our conversations, especially with friends, retain something of the spontaneity of immature expression, but even here saying what we think and feel is often counterproductive.

The hypothesis that the center of gravity shifts from expression to persuasion is almost compelled by certain considerations. The process of decentering involves the increasing ability to anticipate the viewpoints of others and to adjust our discourse accordingly, which means an overall drift toward decoder-centeredness, toward patent or latent suasive intent. Modally, we begin with story, with narration or description, learning to cope with analogic and tautologic much later, the modes indispensable to case making, to mature argument. Finally, the social demands of adulthood require us to function often and extensively as advocates and cajolers, whether at home, at work, or in other settings.

In sum, I think Beale is correct in placing persuasion at the center of the universe of mature, written discourse (113). What he did not see from his perspective and what Britton did not see from his is the developmental shift from expression to persuasion. Instead, Beale denies expression full status as an aim (83), a bad move from any point of view. It is hard to see how we can handle the discourse of children without expression; and if there is little expression in adult writing, then expression, relatively speaking, goes

underground—to conversation, private writing, and other unpublished out-
lets (e.g., therapy sessions).

The hypothesis of a shift in the center of gravity from expression to
persuasion as we move from the early stages of literacy to mature literacy
is only descriptive in intent. It may help us to see certain patterns in discourse
development. But even if the hypothesis is borne out by empirical reflection,
its normative or pedagogical implications are at least problematical. Perhaps
we should swim against the current, paying special attention to expressive
discourse in the later years of formal education on the grounds of, say,
good self-therapy and better interpersonal understanding. Or perhaps we
should go with the current, helping to develop the kind of discourse adults
need and encounter most—persuasion. In my experience, most college students and most college graduates are inept at rational inquiry, case construction, and analysis of discourse appealing for their assent. Nor is this
surprising, given the decline in the older, rhetorical model of education,
the prestige of reference discourse, and the continuing domination of literature in English studies.

What we should do, then, even if my descriptive hypothesis has some
validity, is far from clear. Valid or not, however, our goal should be writing
in all the aims. For this reason, and because even a hint of privilege for one
aim or another leads to endless and pointless disputes about which aim is
more important and most deserving of instruction, it is wise to adhere to
Kinneavy's nonevaluative model, his neutral grounding of the aims of discourse in the communication triangle.

Context

As with media, all our theorists are aware of the context variable, but none
of them carry its analysis very far. Kinneavy reminds us of the traditional
distinction between context of text and context of situation, using both,
especially the latter, to interpret his example texts; he concentrates on context from a product-criticism point of view. Britton is more interested in
the act of writing and in the difference between speech contexts and text
contexts. Probably because of Vygotsky he sees speech as a fully dramatic
act, utterance on a stage, within a context of time and place, interlocutor
and audience, and he sees writing as dramatic at one remove, creating an
explicit context within the text and fictionalizing a readership. Britton calls
attention to the special sense and demands of context in writing, leaving
us with a deeper awareness of what a young writer must learn somehow
to approach mature competence in the medium. Finally, Moffett deals with
context in an expanded sense when he situates all discourse acts in other

discourse acts. His point is not just that all writing is built on prior writing by the author and others but also, and more emphatically, that the oral and the written interact, discussion feeding writing and vice versa, a process of exchange Moffett's dramatic classroom would do everything to encourage.

Obviously, context is a multifaceted concept. The following descriptions discriminate its various uses:

Context of culture: the equivalent of *world* as I have used this term; also the equivalent of *horizon* in hermeneutics; designates the shared knowledge, beliefs, and values of a language community; mostly tacit, unquestioned, foundational in the sense of furnishing a discourse's assumptions and presumptions.

Context of discourse: the situatedness of all discourse in past discourse; overlaps with context of culture, but more local and specific in referring to one's place or role in an ongoing argument, tradition, or group within a language community; may also designate discourse behind or preparatory to one's own, such as discussion or research, making it a part of the composing or precomposing process.

Context of situation: the felt need to speak or write, whether arising as an impulse from within, as a demand from without, or by a combination of the two; marks the beginning of the composing process; designates what I have heretofore called the expressive impulse, when the felt need to speak or write comes more from within than without.

Context of text: designates situatedness of an utterance or a written assertion within a conversational exchange, a speech, or text; the place of an excerpted passage in the discourse from which it is taken; a prime source of motive or constraint on the drafting process, since what one is about to say or write must connect with what has already been said or written and with what one projects beyond the current focus of utterance or inscription.

I offer this four-category breakdown of context for pragmatic purposes only, as an effort to reduce the ambiguity of the term itself. Although the categories move from the relatively general and abstract to the relatively specific and concrete, they otherwise lack systematic justification; moreover, sharp boundaries cannot be drawn between them. My only claim is exhaustiveness; I have encountered no use of the term *context* by discourse theorists that falls outside my analysis.

More important than any division of context is how we think with the concept itself. For many, *context* implies something objective or quasi-objective, an external set of conditions that are just there, a given, like fate and the weather. Closely related is a further implication, that context is static, perhaps the result of using monolithic abstractions like "Western culture" and "*the* literary tradition," Platonic essences, fixed and imperious. The truth is that context is never objective and never static; rather, it is an ongoing process of interpretation.

The chief reason for this is that we have no unmediated grasp of the out there, no immediate intuition of how things are. What we call culture is nothing more than a predisposition to construe experience according to past habits and rationalizations. The human condition is summed up in Martin Heidegger's "thrownness" (Linge xlvii–xlviii): We always find ourselves in context, with no way out of or above the interpretative systems that happen to prevail in our time and place.

We never, therefore, have reality; instead, we have an interpretation of reality. Likewise, to use the term *context* without distortion entails never forgetting its inescapably mediate or interpretative nature; context is neither in here (subjective) nor out there (objective) but an intersubjective construction of the meaning and value of human experience. Consequently, it is never fixed; it is dynamic.

If all meanings of context are intersubjective and dynamic rather than objective and static, what conclusions or attitudes follow from this premise? Most important, no deterministic or quasi-deterministic view of context is acceptable; we cannot deduce or predict the nature of a discourse from knowledge of its context, as Lloyd F. Bitzer purports in his celebrated essay "The Rhetorical Situation" (6). First, we have no privileged access to context but only our interpretation of it, which will certainly differ from the author's and that of other interpreters. Second, even if the context is relatively obvious, so simple and straightforward that virtually everyone assesses it in the same way, a speaker or a writer may fail to respond to exigence through sheer ineptitude or may choose to defy contextual expectations for perfectly good reasons, perhaps to protest the conventional response to a particular situation. Finally, even if intersubjective agreement about context is high, and even if the speaker or writer is skilled, primed for the task at hand, and willing to concede to conventional expectation, any student of rhetorical tactics could probably suggest a range of satisfactory choices that would more or less satisfy exigential demands. Here the piece of folk wisdom about many ways to skin a cat surely applies.

If our object, then, is to explain a particular discourse, knowledge of context alone is at most weakly predictive, a source of inference in need of the other variables for anything approaching a satisfactory account. It is no bedrock notion, no court of ultimate hermeneutic appeal. Quite the contrary; we are always working with our interpretations of an author's interpretations of context, so that typically context itself becomes fundamentally disputed. As with attributions of aim, so also with context: we can only make our best case, trusting that the give-and-take of critical opinions will ultimately yield the most plausible construction.

The disputable or negotiable nature of context is as evident from the teaching or process angle as it is from the criticism or product viewpoint. I believe, however, that too often context is treated in our texts and presented to our students as if it were objective and static; too often we impose a context, assuming that the implications of our interpretation are self-evident. What we need to do instead is show our students how differently the "same context" is constructed by writers and how much varying constructions influence tactics. We need to explore contexts with them, challenging the self-evident interpretations that frequently prove just unimaginative. And, of course, as Britton points out, the peculiar nature of the writing medium requires that we teach our students how to create an explicit context within our texts, how to frame what we say so that our interpretations of context are recognized and shared by our readers as closely as possible.

To sum up thus far, context at every level is an interpretation—intersubjective, dynamic—a construct that may require rational defense. This is so even at the level of context of text, which seems so solidly there: but it too is a construction, since people differ over whether or not a passage was taken out of context.

Turning now to the implications of context for this theoretical synthesis, we encounter a number of potential problems—most notably how to limit a concept that not only overlaps the territory of the other variables but also manifests an imperialistic tendency to swallow them whole. Otherwise put, What isn't context? Spontaneously we think and speak of a contrast between a "me in here" and a "they/it out there," container and contained, scene and agent in Burke's dramatistic calculus (*Grammar* 3). And clearly a contrast of some sort is required for the concept of context: context must contain something that is not context. If everything is context, nothing is context.

We are discussing what George Lakoff would term the "cognitive model" of context, its underlying "logic" or dialectic, based on a metaphor of container and contained, itself based in turn on the bodily sense of a distinction between "me" and "the world" (271–73). Without such a model, context is nonsense. And yet, what is me or mine? Not the culture-bearing language I use, which I had to acquire and learn from others, not the discourse conventions (aims, genres, modes, media), which belong to the language community into which I was thrown at birth; not even me is mine, for everybody's *I* comes from the collective store of roles, attitudes, and values.

What isn't context, then? Nothing. But if everything is context, the very concept is dissolved or deconstructed, rendered meaningless. The in here is the out there and vice versa, container equals contained. And so it must be. For we can draw no line between scene and agent, scene and act. Context is in this sense a fiction, a construct, an interpretation based on human cognition. We must not expect it to correspond necessarily to anything in reality: in reality everything is context, even the genetic material that makes everyone but identical twins biologically unique; in any event, *in reality* is itself a construct, an interpretation, making any final, authoritative matching of concept and referent impossible.

We see from another angle why we must resist the objective feel of context. But given the dialectic of the concept partially discussed above, how do we handle context? First, clearly, we should give over any effort to separate context from the other variables, except as an analytic convenience of greater or lesser utility. Second, we must work with context as it is felt by writers and readers; we must take seriously its variability, the shifting limen between tacit context and conscious context. Put another way, although we often speak of writers and texts as having contexts, it is probably less misleading to say just the opposite, that contexts have writers and texts. But most of this having is tacit, not felt by anyone in the process of composing, or reading, or interpreting, or criticizing. Tacit context is our second nature, so ubiquitous, so completely internalized that we instinctively resist it as an interpretation; we claim to approach a text or a writing task with an open mind, but our very openness depends on the subconscious foreknowledge we bring to every reading and writing act.

Felt, or conscious, context, therefore, takes in the very little that we happen to have in mind as we write or read—that part of context no longer tacit because we can formulate it for ourselves or for others. What is felt at any time depends, obviously, on a host of factors, too many to permit more than illustration: the writer's intelligence; quantity, range, and depth of experience; energy available for the project at hand; commitment to or interest in it; the current focus of the public mind or of a particular discipline; the kind of discourse, since, for example, dialectical questioning tends to bring to consciousness certain aspects of foreknowledge not exposed for us before; the medium, because what is salient for the speaker, with an audience present in a well-defined occasion, may not be salient for the writer working in a study. And so on. I can imagine no variable that we might isolate for discussion in a discourse theory that would not have some impact on the shifting limen between tacit and conscious context.

The distinction between tacit and conscious context helps to clarify part of our role as teachers–editors in the writing class. Besides assisting students in the formulation of felt contexts and in exploring the implications of opposing interpretations, we need also to bring to light aspects of tacit context relevant to the task at hand. Such consciousness-raising occurs naturally as we discuss the other variables, since context overlaps with all of them, especially reader, medium, and aim.

I hope this exploration of context has established two main points: that context is a construction, an interpretation, and is therefore not objective but always to some degree open and negotiable; that context as a construct always has a vast substructure and is greatly in need of exploration, especially as one prepares to write. From a purely synthetic viewpoint, what I have tried to do is integrate terminology from Kinneavy with the dynamic, intersubjective view of context one finds in Moffett and Britton, but I have pushed it harder and farther than they chose to take it.

Perhaps some readers will feel that I have offered them no clear idea of context. That is regrettable, because I sought—to paraphrase Langer—a definite center of meaning for the concept, even though I found mostly its labile limits, its tendency to merge with other variables. Part of the problem is that context is polysemous, and consequently any arbitrary effort to distill it, while useful in an ad hoc way, might be theoretically suspect. It is also difficult to gain a secure purchase on something that we are always in the midst of—what water is for a fish, context is for human beings. Even the desire to have clear ideas is part of our context of culture, so that any serious effort to grapple with context rapidly takes on the confusing reflections upon reflections that T. S. Eliot expressed so well as a "wilderness of mirrors" (21).

Perhaps the most workable simplification for praxis is to radiate from context of situation. It is here we would probably begin anyway in pondering context, since the variable itself takes on dimension once we have defined a writing task or had it defined for us. If this is the relative center of what we mean by context in writing, we must nevertheless remember that no context of situation can exist without context of discourse and culture. At best, then, to set out from context of situation is only to begin, to establish a field for the play of our variables, all of which are distinct and not distinct from the idea of context itself. What counts ultimately is not drawing sharp lines between our variables but exploiting their dialectical interaction in the writing process.

Summation: The Act Variables

Aim as a judgment is indispensable to discourse theory, aiding interpretation of finished discourses or drafts and serving as part of the guiding gestalt, or sense of the whole, that writers develop before or during the process of writing. As a heuristic concept, aim also helps in sorting out genres that exist in a particular time and place; without genre we cannot arrive at the level of typical features or norms characteristic of genuine discourse classes. The linking of aim with genre, then, allows us to recognize motives shared by discourses with quite different surfaces and to specify discourse classes sufficiently to talk about shared features such as logic, organization, and style. The two concepts work and belong together.

Another close linkage are the variables subject matter and mode. In the final analysis, subject matter can be recognized in a theory of discourse but not specified; the variable itself can only be handled by teaching writing in all disciplines and subdisciplines—by writing across the curriculum. Likewise, the modes or means of discourse, including special logics and other languages, can be taught with full effectiveness only by specialists in the various disciplines, those who have actually struggled with the concrete demands of the subject matter. However, it is possible at an admittedly high level of abstraction to recognize basic intellectual processes that will be discoverable in any extended discourse act. For this purpose I have advocated Moffett's treatment of the I–it relation, which includes Kinneavy's modes even while moving several steps beyond them. To be more useful, Moffett's modes, especially analogic, need a great deal more development both in themselves and in relation to such concepts as topics of invention.

The media variable received comparatively little attention in our four theories. Something approaching a full theory of media would have to reckon systematically with primary orality, writing, print, and secondary orality (including film, television, radio—all the electronic media). For our purposes the complex relation between orality and literacy matters the most: while contrasting them helps to reveal the discrepant demands of writing and speaking (especially conversation), integrating them is the prime goal of writing instruction, since writing builds on and tends to stimulate dialogue. The move from orality to literacy has enormous impact on conceptual ability generally and, together with other forces of acculturation, results in persuasion's replacing expression as the center of gravity in mature discourse.

Context, the fourth and last of the act variables, designates four distinguishable but overlapping notions: contexts of culture, of discourse, of situation, and of text. All are interpretations, not objective facts. Probably the most important point to remember about context is that most of it is at all times tacit or latent. A small part of it is conscious or felt as we write, so that the central hermeneutical task where context is concerned is to help students become aware of and to question as much of the tacit context as possible. Particular writing tasks are probably illuminated most steadily and directly by attention to the implications of situational context.

We turn now from the variables of the act to the actors: writer, reader, and editor. The first two are implicit in the communication triangle as encoder and decoder; the third, while an agent of central importance in much writing, is largely neglected in our theories of discourse and pedagogy.

THE AGENT AND PROCESS VARIABLES

The Agent Variables: Writer, Editor, Reader

Our view of the agent variables can be very complex or quite simple. As actual individuals responding to one another at various phases in the composing process, the relationships are as rich and complex as the individuals involved and their opportunities for dialogue over an evolving text. But as players wearing masks, as formalized roles, the relationships become relatively flat and obvious. The writer-reader relation, Britton point out, is a reciprocal relation, each implying the other: if the writer takes the role of expert, the reader becomes the uninformed lay person; if a novelist begins, as Hemingway often does, in media res with many unexplained references to very definite props and events that we are apparently supposed to know about, then we the readers must cast ourselves as the writer's companions. As for the person in the middle, the editor, usually undetectable in the text but looming somewhere behind it, that agent is a quality assessor, market evaluator, revision taskmaster—a kind of broker between author and reader.

The agent variables, then, are at least two-leveled, one richly human, spontaneous, as unpredictable as our best friends, the other an elegant, three-sided dance the formality of which is dictated by partners who scarcely know one another and who therefore must keep their distance. And yet only conceptually are the two levels distinct: they merge and depart in the actual process of composing. For example, a writer does work with a fictive readership in the Britton-Ong sense, creating an appropriate role in the text for all those unknown others that may conceivably read it; but writers also write for a few intimate friends or colleagues, who are perhaps vaguely representative of the audience out there, but whose function it is to respond to the manuscript before going public, before the broker finds the text in the mail. So the two levels, both distinct and not, really interact. They may also alternate in the same person, as in the friend or colleague who happens also to be an editor and who responds to our text from both angles.

What about the agent variables in the classroom? The Britton study confirmed what everyone knows about almost all school writing—that the intended reader is the teacher, a state of affairs Britton and many others have strongly decried. If school writing should approximate real writing in the world, surely the most appropriate role for the teacher is not reader but editor. The teacher is a poor "fictive reader" because very little mature, published writing is for a single individual—Britton's "internalized other"—but is rather for some segment of the reading public—Britton's "generalized other." Nor is the teacher a peer, a colleague whom the student writer would naturally approach for a first reading. The teacher's authority in the classroom more nearly resembles that of the real-world editor found in business, journalism, and book publishing. The teacher should be a broker between the student writer and a genuine segment of the reading public. Even the teacher's role as grade giver, which causes so much artificial strain in the classroom, accords with the editor's responsibility for deciding whether or not to publish, and if to publish, whether or not to revise. In short, the teacher is an evaluator with much the same authority as the editor.

While the two roles are scarcely a perfect fit, rational assessment assigns an editor's role to the teacher. No other even approximates authenticity. But playing this role entails altering the school writing game appreciably. As the saying goes, old habits die hard: students who have been rewarded for outsmarting their teachers will begin a draft for an announced audience and then after a paragraph or a page revert to the teacher as reader; the teacher, accustomed to being the student's reader, will struggle to respond consistently and helpfully to a draft written for a little-known readership. The new dance may prove awkward at first; a teacher will sometimes revert to praising or criticizing a passage as if he or she were the intended reader rather than the editor. But the value of the teacher as editor makes adjustment easier; moreover, taking this role and insisting on it may provide exactly the impetus needed for students to relinquish the relative security of the internalized other and write at last for the audience adults envision for publication, the generalized other, a readership corresponding roughly to some definite existing group.

In theory the teacher is an editor, but can we assume this role in practice? We cannot if our classes are too large, since editing requires one-on-one dialogue. Furthermore, only an experienced, confident teacher, one possessing the necessary acuity and commitment, will be able to sustain the editorial role; otherwise, authority and authenticity will remain wanting.

Much depends on our students—where they happen to be in their development. As Britton points out, writing for a genuine readership requires seeing in one's own work "general value and validity, a readiness to conform with or contribute to some cultural norm or trend, and identification with an audience not personal" (72)—an orientation not always found in teachers, much less students.

Let us now take a closer look at the variables of writer and reader. Those familiar with the controversies in contemporary literary criticism know that one group of rhetorical critics emphasizes the writer's side of the transaction while another emphasizes the reader's. While good cases have been advanced for both, while criticism can be practiced from either perspective, the very nature of writing as a medium or technology makes the writer-reader relation asymmetrical, since the latter must be fictionalized and only the former can do the fictionalizing.

The speaker-auditor relation in oral discourse comes closer to functional equality than the writer-reader relation. Even in formal oratory the audience is present, with input through applause, silence, murmurings, facial expressions, and the like. In conversation the roles become as symmetrical as they can possibly be, since speaker and auditor in turn exchange functions. But in written discourse, the reader's response (assuming the simplest case of writing intended for a single person) is sometimes delayed in time and rendered more indirect by separation in space, since writer and reader may not reside in the same place.

Because of the degree of physical separation, the writer must typically construct the reader to a far higher degree than the speaker has to. Hence the relation between writer and readership is inherently asymmetrical, the readership existing first as a writer's representation, as an intended reader, and then, from the first draft on, as an implied reader, implicit in subject matter, level of diction, syntactic complexity, what is explained and what is not, and so forth. Whether intended or implied, however, readership must be approached through the writer and in terms of the writer, either by conception or by textual choices.

At this juncture perhaps common sense wants to say, "But there really are real readers, and their actual responses matter." While true, this assertion misses a key point: no actual reader involved in the writing process can be simply equated with the readership. The teacher-editor is a reader whose job, so far as the agent variables are concerned, is to assist the writer in conceiving an appropriate intended reader and to scrutinize the text to ensure that intended reader and implied reader mesh. The first-line or test readers consulted by both writers and editors matter, since their comments can alter the text appreciably, but they are not the readership. We must routinely distinguish what is representative in their response from what is idiosyncratic, heeding only the former.

Certainly, then, actual readers exist and their responses matter, but readership, like aim and context, is an interpretation, an abstract, generic concept that must correspond to some segment of the reading public (another abstract, generic concept), but not necessarily to any actual reader. The readership is usually obvious, so strongly implicit in subject matter, aim, medium, and context that nothing one could call a choice enters the picture. If there is a choice, it is almost always within a narrow range. On those rare occasions when significant interpretative differences do arise, normally writer and editor negotiate a working concept, trusting the test readers for verification.

To say that readership is usually obvious is not to say that it is usually simple, merely a matter of the writer assuming one role, with the reader in the role that best complements the writer's. While reciprocal roles are basic to defining a writing task, we can easily oversimplify the general notion of readership, especially if we are thinking mainly of examples drawn from fiction. Ong's classic article does center on literary examples, which for all their subtlety do not expose the chief complicating factor, multiple readerships. Much, perhaps even most, nonfiction writing produced outside academe has several readerships in mind, a fact well known to technical writers and technical writing teachers but otherwise not widely recognized by most composition instructors. So diverse are the readerships for many company reports that separate parts are written for the technical staff, the research division, the executives, and so on. Outside business, probably the commonest multiple readerships are the two we find, for example, in "Letter from Birmingham Jail": a nominal readership explicitly addressed by the author and a larger public readership whom the author also hopes to reach but seldom addresses.

The problem of multiple readerships belongs to advanced college writing courses; how can we teach readership in general, at and below this level? We can certainly structure assignments so that the teacher is not the reader; in this way perhaps we can avoid what Britton calls "pseudoinformative writing," discourse that proves to a teacher that a student knows something but that does not inform because the teacher knows it already. Better yet, we can explore possible readerships with our students; given, say, the persuasive aim, students can ask themselves the following questions: Who out there really cares about this issue? Who has taken what position on it and how have they argued? Which group or groups do I have a chance of persuading? If my essay could be published, where would I send it and who would read that publication? Such questions can help students discover and isolate the characteristics of their intended readership.

We can also insist that our students find appropriate first-line readers to respond to their work at the first or second draft phase. No doubt we will often need to provide a checklist for such readers, just as professional editors do; no doubt we will have to work with students on how to respond to the responses, how to see what is valuable in the critiques, and how to go about altering their texts to incorporate valid criticisms. Beyond this, our continuing task is to sensitize students to implied readerships in everything written. They must see what even the most advanced undergraduates do not usually perceive, that even a short note written on the run has an implied readership, a certain "recipe" of explained and unexplained references, stylistic choices, tone and stance, all of which, taken together, will allow us to construct the implied reader. Students need to be shown in detail the implied readers of their texts, especially when implied fails to align with intended readership. They need to practice editing and revising texts for different intended readerships. The opportunities to teach readership are available whenever we study anything textual, and we must seize these opportunities on the sound principle that students will never grasp the abstract and hypothetical notion of readership as long as readership itself remains invisible, in the background, unattended to.

Reader-response theory has advanced many concepts of the reader (Mailloux). Whether a readership is fictive, intended, implied, or nominal, it is always a hypothetical genus, an interpretative construct, except, perhaps, when we are writing for someone we know very well. Even then, some synthesizing of the reader goes on, the difference between intimate other and generalized other being a matter of degree more than of kind. We share more with the intimate other, know more, have a better chance to test our hypotheses about that intimate other, but we must construct.

The writer likewise is someone not just there but "created"—the mask, the persona, the tone and stance adopted for this particular task, created by the writer and re-created by the reader. Everyone is constantly in the process of self-making; there is no fixed "I" but a dynamic interplay of otherness, an inner dialogue of internalized voices. My I is plural, a "corporate 'we,'" as Kenneth Burke phrases it (*Attitudes* 264). My sense of "me" as perduring sameness, as an identity, results from the centrality of the nervous system, the present structure of what I have taken in, my self-interpretations and the perceptions of others, and a unique genetic inheritance. My sense of me is not therefore illusory, just not one sense or a sense decreed for all time. If the writer's audience is a fiction, likewise the writer is a fiction, in part a deliberate fabrication but mostly a construct of experiences too deeply internalized for conscious control.

As human beings, as complex, dramatic selves, writer and reader are on a par, symmetrical; we experience this equality when we talk with actual readers about something we have written. But in all other respects, the writer–reader relation is asymmetrical. Readers are implied by texts; the writer confronts us through the text, making assertions, directing our attention, assuming for us a certain presence—a voice, a tone, a stance, a style. A readership is a genus; the writer is a concrete individual, a person with a biography. Ultimately the reader only cooperates with a text to make meaning; the writer is responsible for and answerable to the text.

I mention these obvious but deep-seated asymmetries as a way of explaining why rhetoricians from Aristotle to E. D. Hirsch have always emphasized the author's side of the transaction. I agree with Gadamer that texts require readers for the dialogue to begin: I can confront no one, I have no textual presence of any kind without a reader (*Truth* 340). But the asymmetries inherent in writing irresistibly foreground the writer. While reading is an art in itself and practicing critics have a legitimate interest in their own processes, the art of rhetoric has always been for writers and orators. Aristotle's definition of rhetoric even suggests that success in the art is a matter not of how actual audiences respond but of the speaker's skill in discovering and deploying the available means of persuasion (Cooper 6–7). Likewise, our concern is primarily the writer's art, the writer's skill in achieving a particular aim for an intended or fictive readership.

What I am advocating, in sum, is a double perspective. On the one hand, the agent variables are all on the same level, dramatic selves interacting in the total writing process; on the other hand, the writer *is* the rhetorician, the very center of rhetorical praxis. We can justify treating the writer as foremost among equals by appealing to the asymmetries inherent in chirography and print, and we will probably have to take the writer's part given the current fashion of seeing texts solely in terms of other texts, amid talk of the "disappearance" not only of the writer but of any kind of presence outside of texts. Detachment of text from its maker is, of course, only one consequence of deconstructionist thought, but it is enough in itself to expose its fundamentally antirhetorical position. Our task is "reconstructionist," for we cannot practice the art of rhetoric with "traces," with mere *différance*, but only with human beings, whose exercise of the art makes a difference (Derrida 57, 166, 168; Rabinow 101–20).

If saving the author from dispersion into textuality means saving rhetoric from reduction to traces, it also preserves the richest variable among the agents in the writing process. The writer, this unique combination of human genetics and internalized otherness, is a locus of motives without which we cannot function, whether as rhetoricians, editors, or critics. We know, for example, from intuition and experience that Britton is right about the impact of attitude on both products and processes of literacy. But how can we discuss perfunctory, involved, and impelled apart from writers who have such attitudes? (Readers possess the same attitudes, but not in a way that directly affects rhetorical art.) Likewise, the writer has a certain level of linguistic competence, of emotional and intellectual maturity, of experience with and immersion in literacy, of openness or closedness to the teacher-editor, to peers, and to the world beyond daily experience—all of which figure directly in explaining a finished text or one in process. And finally, certain traditional rhetorical terms depend utterly on the writer's being foremost among equals. For example, *stance*, attitude toward one's readership, resides in the writer, as does *tone*, attitude toward subject matter. Such notions are critical to understanding both product and process, and while they derive ultimately from transpersonal sources, from otherness, from social or communal norms, and thus do not belong to any one writer, they enter into rhetoric on both the felt and tacit levels.

The writer may be a fiction, but he or she is a necessary fiction in Wallace Steven's strong sense, a sine qua non. There can be no rhetorical art without an artist, no rhetorical act without an agent-maker. Our dialectic of discourse variables cannot function without it; human intercourse itself cannot function apart from the I-you relation's overcoming of the alienating "it" of textuality.

The Process Variables: Composing and Precomposing

Fitting together what our four theorists have to say about process is a relatively easy task, since each develops an aspect of the notion and none of the various aspects seriously conflict. All we need to do is collect their contributions and articulate connections among them—or at least that fulfills the task of synthesis. As in previous sections, my intent is to move the discussion beyond the needs of synthesis per se; in this instance, I hope to open up the question of process with a few reflections of my own.

Process in Kinneavy is history, the history of discourse types and of discourse instruction—our tradition. But the term *process* for us does not by and large mean history; rather it means the composing process, and so we see the static categories, the analyses of finished discourses, the lack of a composing model, and conclude that *A Theory of Discourse* is simply product-oriented. Relative to present perspectives, relative to our other theories, it is product-oriented, but to the extent we fail to appreciate the process-as-history dimension in Kinneavy we reveal our own blindness, not his.

What does "appreciate" mean here? Not, I hope, the usual superficial justifications for historical study, which make of it a distanced object, like old furniture displayed in a museum, roped off to make sure we do not sit on or touch it. Nor is history merely cautionary—so many lessons to be learned—or merely chastening, as when we discover that an idea we thought original only reinvents the wheel. Rather, history *is* what we are, even if we know nothing about it, for history is embedded in our language, and language carries the culture we internalize. What we vaguely refer to as the historical process has a concrete, everyday presence in our lives, directly relevant to composition. Context of culture is history, the source of convention, of habitual ways of seeing and acting, the source of meaning itself. Out of it come our horizons, our framework for every interpretation. History is the foreknowledge we bring to every act of reading, the foreknowledge that permits us to recognize and interpret situational contexts. It is inseparable from discourse because discourse makes history and makes us.

Full appreciation of process in the sense of history is difficult for us. We think of it as a mere subject area, perhaps part of an area exam, under "history of rhetoric." It is the concern of certain specialists, like Kinneavy, Kennedy, Corbett, Vickers. For us, for Americans, the problem is especially acute, since for us history has always been, at a visceral level, bunk. The American myth is starting over, at its origin a desire to break with tradition. In our small and local way we are reenacting the myth, defining ourselves by dissociation from the old ways, the anathema of the product orientation, for which we would substitute various "new" rhetorics, most of which are just revamped old ones. The very idea of history presented in the last paragraph is European, its distant source Hegel, its more recent source Heidegger, its clearest expositor Gadamer.

Regardless of the way we perceive history—as prior, isolated events that we as educated people are obliged to know (otherwise we may fail Hirsch's culture test) or as Gadamer's *Wirkungsgeschichte* 'effective history' working itself out now in our every thought and deed (*Philosophical Hermeneutics* 13, 27)—we must, I think, agree to this: not a single discourse variable exists as a disembodied, timeless, placeless notion, a Platonic idea. All emerged somewhere, evolved a certain way, and are therefore part of our thinking now, still evolving in our dialogues about them. And that includes, of course, the very notion of process itself. Kinneavy's focus, then, on the history of our leading ideas is not only valuable for self-understanding and a corrective to those who know little about rhetoric before the 1960s; it is also the most embracing notion of process that we have.

Britton, in contrast to Kinneavy, has little to say about process in the sense of history; rather, his focus is the "Emig and after" sense of process as "the composing process," indisputably the central notion of contemporary composition praxis. I have already indicated my sympathy with

Britton's careful, questioning approach to process in the sense of composing; the following observations are not directed to Britton so much as they are to the general notion of the composing process that he helped to popularize and that seems to me in need of a friendly critique.

The first difficulty connected with the general notion is that it implies a whole range of allegiances sloganized as the "process approach" and conceived too often in flat, simplistic opposition to the "product approach." The slogan is useful for group identity, but dangerous insofar as it leads to false dichotomizing. As noted before, process and product mutually imply each other; one cannot think long and hard about either without also thinking about its opposite. More concretely, from the time we write our first sentence, product and process interact; the "already said" conditions the "yet to be said." As Britton observes, writing depends on scanning back; the being, or succession of temporary states, is always present in becoming, in the next shaping at the point of utterance (35). Such is the dialectic at work, which dissociation of product from process can conceal from view.

Clearly, then, every process approach must grapple with products, and even the most incorrigibly old-fashioned approach to teaching composition (represented for me by the writer of a well-known, bestselling handbook who was very proud of having memorized the reference numbers in his text, allowing him to save much ink and time by scribbling things like "18.2" in the margins of student papers) inevitably intervenes in the composing process. Perhaps the intervention is too late, too exclusively concerned with correctness, and too magisterial to do the student much good, but the product approach is also, willy-nilly, processual. If we refuse to accept the product-process dichotomy, and in so doing also question the false impression of univocity implicit in the process approach, we stand a better chance of approaching the concept itself in a more clearheaded manner.

The next step is to come to terms with the mighty hypostatization "the composing process." It doesn't actually exist, of course, as studies of actual writers in the act of writing confirm. What we find is tremendous variation, not only from individual to individual, but also from task to task. Yet we go on constructing abstract models of the composing process and refining these models and presenting them to our students, even though they fit no one writing anything in particular. We have created a myth, the unreality of which is only confirmed by all the warnings about individual and task variation issued by the composing theorists themselves.

The problem is rooted in our approach to the composing process. This approach has been, as Burke would say, "too scientistic." We have abstracted it from the writing act, reified it into an entity, and, following the compulsive logic of such thinking, treated it as if it had a life and a structure of its own. We have sought to know and to master it, to control and to predict. And we have encountered one of the persistent backlashes of such thought: when we try to apply it, insert it into reality, nothing works as it did "under laboratory conditions." How could it? Our first step was to isolate, to abstract away from the reality in which the so-called composing process was embedded: lack of fit is inherent in the very way of proceeding.

Because lack of fit is inherent, I think we must seek an alternative to the prevailing scientistic approach to composing. We must find another way of thinking. And that means finding a better analogy than Emig and her followers have pursued, which likens the composing process to discovery in general, to preparation, incubation, illumination. Some, perhaps even the most valuable, writing is a genuine act of discovery; but most is not, and much of discourse presenting such genuine acts is *re*constructive of an act of discovery that transpired in precomposing (in thought, dialogue, scientific inquiry, etc.) rather than in the composing process proper.

An alternative to scientism is dialectical or dramatistic thinking. A better analogy or informing metaphor is dialogue, or what Gadamer calls the buoyancy of playing a game, of "giving one's self over" to the act itself (*Philosophical Hermeneutics* 57). The central idea is that composing is not something we can or need to understand. The question of what really goes on when we write is fascinating but secondary, for grasping composing counts for little if we are not grasped by it. All we know or can know about the physiology, psychology, sociology, or phenomenology of writing can have no significant impact on anything without a certain quality of engagement. If most of our students opt out, refusing genuine commitment, playing the game only in the sense of psyching out the teacher for a grade, all we can tell them about writing has exactly the same relevance as an excellent lecture-demonstration on how to serve presented to someone who doesn't want to play tennis. What makes a writer a writer is serious playfulness, being picked up and carried along by the task at hand, just as one becomes immersed in a dialogue or a game of chess.

No one who has ever taught writing and cared about it would deny the priority of being grasped by composing. Without this quality of engagement, the writing classroom is a shadow play, an energy-draining exercise in despair. That is why our literature is full of "try this," somebody's attempt to share a creative assignment or classroom tactic that at least temporarily turned student writers into real writers. While sometimes helpful, these ad hoc suggestions do not promote genuine commitment. That is what Moffett's dramatistic classroom does and that is why so many of us return again and again to *Teaching the Universe of Discourse*. His dramatistic understanding of composing is tied to the concrete motives of *this* act going on now, rather than to some abstract model of composing that connects with nothing.

Like "discovering the available means of persuasion," the composing process as a whole is completely relative to the given case. It results from a convergence of motives, a dialectical interaction of all the variables discussed in previous sections, but perhaps chiefly the following ones:

1. Writer's intent (aim) and target genre
2. Writer's intended readership(s)
3. Writer's attitude toward the task
4. Writer's level of discourse ability, including cognitive development
5. Writer's discipline, largely a function of degree of maturity
6. Context of situation, all the factors felt as external by writers, such as time and space constraints, relationships with coauthors and editors, institutional and political imperatives

To these variables we need to add two others not yet discussed:

1. Writer's composing style
2. Writer's quantity and quality of immersion in precomposing

I will explain these last two and dilate somewhat on the others as I describe and defend this dramatistic or dialectical understanding of composing.

Instead of dealing with an abstract model of the composing process, we need to grapple with what exists—*a* composing process, the result of a given case, a unique convergence of interacting and conflicting motives. Our responsibility as teachers–editors is to help our students interpret the task at hand and uncover possible strategies for encompassing that task. What might be called tactical hermeneutics is the art of rhetoric. But how do we get a handle on this art?

In an age of facile talk about accountability in education, it is wise to admit at the outset that we can never grasp and control composing, the art of rhetoric. Its foundation, as noted before, is knack, know-how, a vast reservoir of tacit knowledge built up over years of immersion in literacy and thousands of *essais*, trial and error. From this foundation comes foreknowledge, everything we bring to each reading and writing, and which largely determines how well we cope. Finally, inseparable from knack and foreknowledge and not reducible to them is that mysterious something we call talent or natural ability, presumably genetic in origin.

These factors, of course, are given. We can do with them, but we can do nothing about them.

And then there are the variables we can only influence slightly, if at all. A writer's composing style, for instance. As someone who sweats and bleeds out one or two pages a sitting, I have always envied colleagues who can produce an entire first draft of a chapter or an essay in an afternoon. But I cannot work that way. Likewise, no matter how skillful one is at stage-managing a classroom, fundamentally not much can be done about a writer's attitude toward composition in general or toward a particular writing task, about a student's discourse or cognitive ability or lack of discipline. We can set the tone and the standards; we can teach a student how to combine sentences and we can concoct exercises to nurture cognitive ability. But basically all we can do is issue a sincere invitation to join in; we cannot ordain enthusiasm for the writing game. Frequently we must just wait, working patiently with the givens while the student grows up, gains more experience, and somehow finds genuine commitment to written communication.

The givens and near givens have profound impact on any composing process, but they are not central to the art of rhetoric. Rather they are largely preconditions for and constraints on praxis, since without some know-how, foreknowledge, or discourse ability no composing could occur at all. Yet, though largely beyond our reach, even the givens and near givens can at least be partially explicated, understood where understanding helps.

At this point we need to ask what it means to "teach process." It means two commitments primarily. First, we tend to structure our classes very differently from the old lecture-centered regime, where papers were assigned, collected, graded, and returned. In accord with my act-centered, dramatistic conception of writing, our "stage-managing" departs appreciably from procedures in the theme-writing class I took twenty years ago. We may lecture some, but we aspire to putting the chalk down, abandoning the lectern, and working with our students as they are writing or preparing to write. The idea, as Moffett expresses it, is high-quality feedback from teacher and peers as students need it—not only or even primarily as a post mortem over a bleeding text but at every step from initial conception to editing and proofing. The idea is not a model of the composing process but an attempt to build concern with process into the very structure of the class itself. In this way, we need never issue solemn warnings about not waiting until the day before a paper is due to begin composition; we have prestructured away from such procrastination in the first place. A student can still opt out, but the class is not designed to encourage indifference to composing, as confining feedback to a grade on the final draft tended to do. If we are really teaching process, we don't have to talk about process at all. We are doing it.

Stage-managing is better than half the battle. It includes organizing the classroom for interaction not only as the students are composing but also before they compose, in that vast and critical period I have been calling precomposing.

Moffett and D'Angelo are both concerned with process in the precomposing sense. Perhaps Moffett's best insights are into what I have called context of discourse, the relation of this current text-in-the-making to its entire discursive background, including discussion, research, previous writing by the author and others' responses to it, texts from that part of the tradition with which the author identifies, and so on. Moffett's concern with context of discourse specifically centers on classroom stage-managing, in linking assignment with assignment, and especially in integrating oral exploration with writing.

D'Angelo's focus on conceptualization is also largely a precomposing emphasis in that his topoi or heuristic system of categories should stimulate discovery or invention in general, not rhetorical invention specifically. In not being tied to an aim or to any other rhetorical variable that can emerge only with the task itself, his system is really dialectical, designed to aid solo and collective thought, the constant intellectual play of minds driven to written expression.

Clearly Moffett and D'Angelo are ultimately talking about much the same thing, since thought either is or must become discursive to be understood and shared. Dialectical play overlaps context of discourse, being the conscious part of the context, what is on our minds or in our thoughts at a particular time. My larger point, however, is not the relation between Moffett and D'Angelo; it is that both of them contribute to a notion neither discusses explicitly, process in the sense of precomposing.

Contemporary rhetoric both has and has not dealt with precomposing —or perhaps it is better to say that we have been talking about precomposing almost obsessively but with much confusion, so that its significance has not fully come to light. The art of rhetoric, a composing process that seeks the available means to secure a particular aim for a particular readership in a particular situational context (the given case), does not begin, cannot even be said to exist, until we take up a writing task or have one imposed on us. It is only then that we begin to think and act rhetorically. But the energy we bring to the task, the summoned charge that allows us to sustain and focus our rhetorical composition, comes from precomposing, that orientation of all serious, committed writers toward their daily experience, that constant, ongoing preparation to write whether they are actually writing or not. Precomposing includes research of every kind, struggle with problems of general or specialized interest, the thinking through or working out of a general philosophy. It is our line of inquiry, our particular clustering of interests, our preoccupations, the character of our intellectual engagement with experience.

We all know how vital precomposing is. Studies of creativity, of heuristic procedures, of processes of inquiry, of dialogics all attest to our efforts to stage-manage precomposing, to stimulate, if somewhat artificially, that quality of engagement that real writers evince as modus vivendi. Furthermore, we know and may even sometimes admit to ourselves that being caught up in precomposing and composing is much of what literacy means beyond the merely functional and superficial notion of skills. Whether one is caught up or not is the difference between functioning in writing and being a writer, a distinction we may not wish to confront, since it exposes a Rhett Butler–like love of lost causes. Very few of our students will ever be more than functional writers; very few have any sense of an adequate response to our invitation to join in. And so they ask, How many pages must it be? and we think about finding some other line of work.

To quit or dive in is our field's equivalent of the existential question "To be, or not to be," posed every day when we encounter students who don't want to play the game and every month when we pick up our paychecks. No way of understanding composing has much bearing on this decision made over and over; however, we can at least quit fooling ourselves with models of composing that suggest that we have the composing process in hand. Precomposing, no less—and probably more—than composing, varies from writer to writer. We can therefore build recognition of precomposing into the structure of our classes so that the invitation we issue implicitly by our stage-managing offers the full potential of a writer, but we cannot do much more than this. The few that will heed the call will justify our diving in; for the rest, merely the ability to function when they must write is challenge enough.

Teaching process, then, means primarily some version of Moffett's dramatistic classroom, immersion in discourse activities, linked and interrelated. Implicit in this stage-managing and integral to it is the second commitment: the commitment to the art of rhetoric, tactical hermeneutics, largely a matter of dialogue in all phases of composing.

Throughout this study I have tried to reformulate quasi-objective concepts like that of aim so that we may see what they really are, intersubjective constructs, cultural norms for interpretation. My reformulations imply an understanding of rhetoric that goes beyond the application of skills; rhetorical *praxis* is hermeneutics from the writer's point of view, basically the selection of strategies or tactics that build on interpretation of the writer's motives as they relate to the demands of the task at hand. The main role of the teacher-editor is to play Socrates, to ask questions that help students understand their own processes.

What sorts of questions? I can elaborate, but not to some systematic method. There is no model, no algorithm, no inventory of necessary questions; there is only a writer's dialogue within the self and with the act that currently emerges, and there is our attempt at midwifing, joining in the dialogue constructively.

Teaching process involves teaching rhetoric. We cannot teach process by talking about it, nor does teaching rhetoric amount to a series of lectures on invention, arrangement, and style. Moffett is basically right: theorizing about process in general and the rhetorical part of process in particular belongs to books like this and to classes that prepare teachers; we can say everything useful about both for a writing class in an introductory lecture explaining the rationale behind our stage-managing.

Past such orientation, teaching rhetoric must arise in the context of the task at hand. "Teaching" here means questioning, showing our students how to probe the task themselves. Such questioning can be guided by the variables discussed in previous sections. Until we understand our aims, readerships, contexts of situation, and so on, we have nothing to invent, no grounds for employing a particular mode or combination of modes, no criteria for stylistic level in general or for any local stylistic choice. Part of the job of questioning is to bring the discourse variables to conscious attention and to suggest, when necessary, lines of inquiry and research, organizational tactics, stylistic options, and the like that may answer to the task as interpreted. Clearly such questioning can go on at any point in the process, since we conceive and reconceive what we are doing, attempt and reject one set of tactics for another; our joining in as teachers-editors depends on the student's invitation, and what we ask depends on what we confront—this student, this particular set of problems. The more we have method, the less likely we are to join in at the right time; the more we think we know what to ask in advance, the less likely we are to find the right questions. In any case, we must *listen* first and last, listen more than we ask, ask more than we tell. The greatest temptation is to do too much.

Nor is our questioning a simple matter of analyzing the task and enumerating strategies. No task exists per se; the task exists only as an interpretation, and there are always various ways to construe the "same situation." We have always grasped the act before it appears—with foreknowledge, with the enabling and disabling preunderstanding we call experience. So much of our questioning opens up no new angle but only exposes and pursues what the student already knows. So much of our questioning is directed not by the discourse variables per se but by our students' overdetermined understanding of the task. Like everybody else, they think their interpretation is the right and the only one. Sometimes we have to point out alternatives. Even if there were only one way to interpret a rhetorical task, a range of strategies in various combinations will offer other possibilities. Again, our job on the ways-and-means end of things is to suggest possibilities latent in their experiences, strategies they know tacitly but cannot employ without our aid.

Teaching process is stage-managing and dialogue. Theory helps, for otherwise we have little to guide either our structuring of the classroom or our questioning. But the essence of both is diving in or joining in—not mastery, but genuine engagement.

Summation: The Agent and Process Variables

We think about discourse primarily in three ways. It is an act, something done with words. As such, it has one or more central purposes or motives—aims; it is an instance of a certain kind of discourse—genre; it is about something and uses certain means for discussing this something—subject matter and mode; it is either a speech act or a text or some combination of both, transmitted orally or in writing, in print or electronically—media; and it takes place in and responds to some construction of a scene or circumstance—context. We also think of it as something that takes place among persons, the agent slant toward discourse, which includes the variables discussed in the first part of this chapter—writer, reader, and editor. As an act it is an ongoing activity, a process, both those many acts involved in the composing process that would produce the completed act, the product, and everything we do as writers to prepare ourselves to write even when we have no definite project.

To work with the agent variables we must think of them in two different but complementary and interacting ways. On the one hand, writer, reader, and editor are persons, with all that word implies for dialogue over a text; on the other hand, each is a construct, each wears a mask, plays a role in the sociology or drama of composing. So far as real writing is concerned, the teacher's role in the classroom is closest to an editor's. By taking that role whenever possible, we promote student choice of a genuine readership, moving past the internalized other to the generalized other. As an editor rather than a reader, the teacher can also help the student wrestle with the problem of securing a tolerable match between fictive reader and implied reader.

Because no reader represents the readership completely, because readerships are interpretations, hypothetical constructs, the relationship between writer and reader is asymmetrical, writers creating themselves and their readers. Consequently, while criticism has emphasized either reader or writer, rhetoric has always been primarily an art for the encoder, the speaker or the writer. Commitment to rhetoric, therefore, means resisting the "disappearance of the author" as developed in the work of both Foucault and Derrida.

Like context, the term *process* covers a lot of ground. There is process in the sense of history, as in Kinneavy's theory, the history of aims and of discourse theory and education. There is process in Moffett's sense, basically Piaget's focus on cognitive development and its relation to discursive ability. There is process in D'Angelo's sense, dialectical preparation for rhetorical performance. And finally there is process in Britton's sense, in the usual meaning of our profession, the composing process.

In my view we have generally reified the composing process, treating it as an entity, whereas it is actually, in any instance of composition, a unique interaction of the act and agent variables. If one accepts this view, then our concern should be building commitment to process into the activities of a writing class, not talking about it or offering models of it, except in relation to some concrete task. Process should never be divorced from the discourse act; it should be treated dramatistically, not scientistically.

Confusion could also be prevented by distinguishing the composing process from the precomposing process. The process of composing exists only when we engage, or are engaged by, a definite project, an impulse or requirement to speak or write. Everything else that writers do as daily preparation for composing—reading, note taking, discussing, thinking and rethinking—belongs to precomposing.

PARTING NOTES: ON PEDAGOGY AND OTHER MATTERS

With any theory or theoretical synthesis, the most important question to ask is, If I buy into this set of ideas, to what exactly am I committing myself? Ideas often have consequences and implications beyond the imagination of their authors. But I would at least ponder some of the implications and consequences of certain ideas articulated in this study, and trust to others to reveal what I have missed.

The leading idea (if one can call it an idea when it is more a way of being) is commitment to dialogue and dialectic. That preference for one formulation over another is not arbitrary, nor is it solely a matter of cash value; it is rationally justifiable. Even if the preference itself was achieved intuitively, nonrationally, its defense can be critiqued in an ongoing dialogue. At a time when reason is under violent attack, when it is reduced to only will to power, verbal arm-twisting, this synthesis commits one to reason, to dialogical give-and-take. Theory (also under attack because reason is under attack) is lifeless apart from commitment to dialogue and dialectic.

The commitment to reason, however, is not a commitment to theory in the sense of a final synthesis, an ultimate, unquestionable foundation, or even a paradigm. I think we are now farther down the road, closer to a more adequate conceptual grasp of discourse and rhetoric. I also think that the multidimensional, wheels-within-wheels view makes it quite impossible to think we can reach a complete understanding of any of the variables, much less of their interaction. Like Moffett I seek only a strategic gain in concept, not the answer. Mindful that all concepts are unstable and that much of what we know intuitively about both discourse and rhetoric is

always preconceptual, rooted in tacit knowledge and the collective unconscious of a shared language, with this synthesis one commits to a never-
ending theoretical quest in a patient, open-ended spirit. Conceptual grasping
is never a having-in-hand but always a reaching. The circle of the unsaid
surrounds all theory, all critique, all reconstruction and synthesis. Consequently, we will achieve coherence not through a paradigm but from the
quality of our dialogue. As with the composing process, so also with the
theoretical process—the basic commitment is engagement, joining in.

After the commitment to theory itself and to dialectical method, the next
most important allegiance is to the understanding of rhetoric as tactical
hermeneutics. A central assumption of hermeneutics is that there is no
unmediated access to the extramental world, that what we perceive out
there is always already preinterpreted, not only by the selectivity of our
brain and senses but also by our culturally engendered expectations. Because
this assumption seems to me fully warranted, I have sought throughout
this study to reconstruct certain concepts insofar as they retain something
of the objective, "just-there" status of a positivist approach to discourse
and rhetoric. The most salient example of my negotiating was over the
concept of aim. But I tried to show, too, that context is also an interpretation, as are all the agent variables, whose personhood amounts to self-
construction with collective materials. At most, the significant variables of
rhetoric and discourse can only approach quasi-objective status—intersubjective consensus—as in some judgments about any of the variables.

The choice of "tactical hermeneutics" as a synonym for the art of rhetoric
clearly has strong implications and consequences for composition pedagogy.
We can glimpse some of these implications by recalling the current-traditional paradigm. One of the deficits of that model was certainly neglect of
invention. But perhaps its most serious deficiency, one that can survive
more or less intact the recovery of a mechanical approach to invention (such
as a checklist of topics), was its tendency to disenfranchise the student-
writer both rhetorically and politically. Instead of seeing the student her-
meneutically, as an active interpreter of the world whose interpretations
have everything to do with rhetorical choices, someone whose whole way
of understanding and acting is at issue, it treated the student as one would
treat a text, as something with isolatable problems, problems that can be
fixed instrumentally, simply by the application, say, of grammar drills.
Success here is to be measured by the degree of inertness achieved, by the
dependency on the master rule-setter. The political implications scarcely
need to be spelled out.

Put positively instead of negatively, commitment to tactical hermeneutics
is commitment to that pedagogical approach defended by James Berlin as
the social-epistemic approach to teaching composition (478, 488–93). A

writing class should challenge much more than a student's grasp of syntax and commas; at stake is the student's, and the teacher's, entire horizon of meaning, the sense of what has been, is, and can be. It follows that very little of moment is or ought to be settled in advance. The teacher as editor is a negotiator, not a final or ultimate authority. Success here is the degree to which students take the initiative, the adequacy of their interpretations of the task at hand, and the means selected for coping with it. The goal is genuine action, the empowering of the student, not mere conformity to an external standard decreed by an external authority. Once again, the political implications are obvious, and the dialogue that is good for theoretical health is also good for the classroom.

One more commitment deserving notice is to dialectic in the sense of Peter Elbow's "embracing contraries" (327–39). Dialectic in the sense of argument cannot function without analysis, without contrasting concepts. But distinctions too often become dichotomies, especially given the social pressure to define ourselves by dissociation from some other group. The result is that instead of seeing product and process as both distinct and complementary, we see them as mutually exclusive opposites, as if there were really a product approach with no process or a process approach with no product. Whenever we encounter a dichotomy, our commitment should be to overcoming it, to an accommodation of opposites. I tried to do this in my synthesis and elsewhere in this study by treating key discourse variables from both product and process perspectives. If Elbow is right, the accommodation of opposites is as necessary to teaching composition as it is to achieving a more adequate and balanced theory of discourse or rhetoric. The same kind of thought that led Elbow to realize that one cannot choose between two contrary roles—the teacher as midwife or enabler and the teacher as society's representative and therefore the student's judge—should lead us to refuse any flat choice between conceptual opposites. The idea is not to avoid contradiction but rather to court it, to bring the conflict of opposites to light, to reconcile them by finding a place where they can work within the whole. This, too, is part of the dialogue of both theory and practice.

Only a few decades ago, rhetoric and composition in English departments was struggling just to survive, to occupy more than a marginal place in a field dominated by literary studies. That struggle has largely been won. Sometimes, however, battles are still lost. Even in places where peaceful coexistence prevails, few colleagues appreciate rhetoric's 2,500-year-old history and see that rhetoric was for millennia the center of humanistic study, that it gave birth to literary criticism, that it held the honored place in the fledgling English departments of the nineteenth century—that, in short, contemporary rhetoric is only attempting to restore an ancient discipline to something approximating its traditional place. The sense of history, it seems, too often disappears when rhetoric is the topic of discussion. Somehow we become the interloper, the new kid on the block, when in truth literary studies in the contemporary sense was invented at Johns Hopkins not quite a century ago (Parker 4,12).

Nevertheless, though we have grounds for grumbling about the manner and the attitude of acceptance, rhetoric in English is no longer fighting just to hold on. The challenge now is to clean up our act, to find a greater degree of inner coherence. We have historians of rhetoric, theorists, students of rhetoric and literature, empiricists, composition administrators, and writing teachers. But is anyone listening to anyone else? Or do the various specialties within rhetoric fail to connect? Don't we in fact have writing teachers impatient with theory and theorists who have lost sight of praxis? How often do empirical studies fail to engage any significant theory? How often do theories ignore what empirical studies have turned up? Granted, part of the problem is without remedy, since no one can keep up with rhetorical studies even in the minimal sense of reading the literature. But isn't there too much willful isolation?

I have not yet lost enough of my hold on reality to believe that this one book can provide the needed inner coherence. Not any number of books could do that, if I am right in thinking that inner coherence can result only from the quality of dialogue. My aim has been to show by example what dialogue can achieve in the context of commitment to open-ended theorizing. What counts the most is the stake we have in rational critique and synthetic striving. Without these complementary moments dialogue has little point. Without them inner coherence has no chance.

WORKS CITED

Auden, W. H. "In Memory of W. B. Yeats." *Chief Modern Poets of Britain and America*. 2 vols. Ed. Gerald deWitt Sanders et al. Toronto: Macmillan, 1970. 1: 369–71.

Beale, Walter H. *A Pragmatic Theory of Rhetoric*. Carbondale: Southern Illinois UP, 1987.

Berlin, James. "Rhetoric and Ideology in the Writing Class." *College English* 50 (1988): 477–94.

Bitzer, Lloyd F. "The Rhetorical Situation." *Philosophy and Rhetoric* 1 (1968): 1–14.

Britton, James, et al. *The Development of Writing Abilities (11–18)*. Urbana: National Council of Teachers of English, 1975.

Brown, Roger. Introduction. Moffet, *Teaching*.

Burke, Kenneth. *Attitudes toward History*. 3rd ed. Berkeley: U of California P, 1984.

———. *A Grammar of Motives*. Berkeley: U of California P, 1969.

———. *The Philosophy of Literary Form: Studies in Symbolic Action*. 3rd ed. Berkeley: U of California P, 1973.

———. *A Rhetoric of Motives*. Berkeley: U of California P, 1969.

Cooper, Lane, ed. *The Rhetoric of Aristotle*. Englewood Cliffs: Prentice, 1932.

Corbett, E. P. J. "Review of *A Theory of Discourse*." *Freshman English News* 1 (1972): 12.

Crusius, Timothy W. "A Brief Plea for Paradigm and for Kinneavy as Paradigm." *Freshman English News* 12 (1984): 1–3.

———. "A Comment on ' "That we have divided / In three our Kingdom": The Communication Triangle and *A Theory of Discourse*.' " *College English* 49 (1987): 214–19.

D'Angelo, Frank. *A Conceptual Theory of Rhetoric*. Cambridge: Winthrop, 1975.

———. "A Generative Rhetoric of the Essay." *College Composition and Communication* 25 (1974): 388–96.

Derrida, Jacques. *Of Grammatology*. Trans. G. C. Spivak. Baltimore: Johns Hopkins UP, 1976.

Elbow, Peter. "Embracing Contraries in the Teaching Process." *College English* 45 (1983): 327–39.

Eliot, T. S. *The Waste Land and Other Poems*. New York: Harcourt, 1930.

Fogarty, Daniel. *Roots for a New Rhetoric*. New York: Teacher's College, Columbia U, 1959.

Fulkerson, Richard. "Kinneavy on Referential and Persuasive Discourse: A Critique." *College Composition and Communication* 35 (1984): 43–56.

Gadamer, Hans-Georg. *Philosophical Hermeneutics*. Trans. and ed. David E. Linge. Berkeley: U of California P, 1976.

———. *Truth and Method*. New York: Crossroad, 1975.

Halliday, M. A. K., and Rugaiya Hasan. *Cohesion in English*. London: Longman, 1976.

Havelock, Eric. *The Muse Learns to Write: Reflections on Orality and Literacy from Antiquity to the Present*. New Haven: Yale UP, 1986.

———. *Preface to Plato*. Cambridge: Belknap–Harvard, 1963.

Hegel, G. W. F. *Science of Logic*. Trans. A. V. Miller. London: Allen, 1969.

Hunter, Paul. " 'That we have divided / In three our Kingdom': The Communication Triangle and *A Theory of Discourse*." *College English* 48 (1986): 279–87.

Johnson, Wendell. "You Can't Write Writing." *The Use and Misuse of Language*. Ed. S. I. Hayakawa. New York: Fawcett, 1962. 109–15.

Kant, Immanuel. *Critique of Judgement*. Trans. J. N. Barnard. New York: Hafner, 1968.

Kennedy, George A. *Classical Rhetoric and Its Christian and Secular Tradition from Ancient to Modern Times*. Chapel Hill: U of North Carolina P, 1980.

Kinneavy, James L. "A Pluralistic Synthesis of Four Contemporary Models for Teaching Composition." *Reinventing the Rhetorical Tradition*. Ed. Aviva Freedman and Ian Pringle. Conway: L & S, 1980. 37–52.

———. *A Theory of Discourse: The Aims of Discourse*. New York: Norton, 1980.

Kinneavy, James L., John Q. Cope, and J. W. Campbell. *Writing: Basic Modes of Organization*. Dubuque: Kendall–Hunt, 1976.

Kinneavy, James L., William McCleary, and Neil Nakadate. *Writing in the Liberal Arts Tradition: A Rhetoric with Readings*. New York: Harper, 1985.

Knapp, Mark L., and James C. McCroskey. "The Siamese Twins: *Inventio* and *Dispositio*." *Today's Speech* 14 (1966): 17–18, 44.

Kroll, Barry, and Roberta J. Vann, eds. *Exploring Speaking-Writing Relationships*. Urbana: National Council of Teachers of English, 1981.

Kuhn, Thomas S. *The Structure of Scientific Revolutions*. 2nd ed. Chicago: U of Chicago P, 1970.

Lakoff, George. *Women, Fire, and Dangerous Things: What Categories Reveal about the Mind*. Chicago: U of Chicago P, 1987.

Langer, Susanne K. *Feeling and Form: A Theory of Art*. New York: Scribner's, 1953.

———. *Mind: An Essay on Human Feeling*. Vol. 1. Baltimore: Johns Hopkins UP, 1967. 3 vols.

Lauer, Janice M., et al. *Four Worlds of Writing*. 2nd ed. New York: Harper, 1985.

Linge, David E., ed. Introduction. *Philosophical Hermeneutics*. By Hans-Georg Gadamer. Berkeley: U of California P, 1976. xi–lviii.

Mailloux, Steven. "Reader-Response Criticism and Teaching Composition." *Interpretative Conventions: The Reader in the Study of American Fiction*. Ithaca: Cornell UP, 1982. 208–16.

McKeon, Richard, ed. Aristotle's *Poetics*. *The Basic Works of Aristotle*. New York: Random House, 1941. 1455–87.

Moffett, James. *Teaching the Universe of Discourse*. 1968. Boston: Houghton, 1983.

Moffett, James, and Betty Wagner. *Student-Centered Language Arts and Reading, K–13: A Handbook for Teachers*. Boston: Houghton, 1983.

Ong, Walter J. *Orality and Literacy: The Technologizing of the Word*. London: Methuen, 1982.

———. *The Presence of the Word: Some Prolegomena for Cultural and Religious History*. Minneapolis: U of Minnesota P, 1981.

———. "The Writer's Audience Is Always a Fiction." *Interfaces of the Word: Studies in the Evolution of Consciousness and Culture*. Ithaca: Cornell UP, 1977. 53–81.

Parker, William Riley. "Where Do English Departments Come From?" *The Writing Teacher's Sourcebook*. Ed. Gary Tate and E. P. J. Corbett. Oxford: Oxford UP, 1981. 3–15.

Perelman, Chaim, and L. Olbrechts-Tyteca. *The New Rhetoric: A Treatise on Argumentation*. Trans. John Wilkinson and Purcell Weaver. Notre Dame: Notre Dame UP, 1969.

Piaget, Jean. *The Language and Thought of the Child*. Cleveland: Meridian, 1955.

Polanyi, Michael. *Personal Knowledge: Towards a Post-Critical Philosophy*. Chicago: U of Chicago P, 1962.

Rabinow, Paul, ed. *The Foucault Reader*. New York: Pantheon, 1984.

Richards, I. A. *The Philosophy of Rhetoric*. Oxford: Oxford UP, 1936.

Rueckert, William. *Kenneth Burke and the Drama of Human Relations*. 2nd ed. Berkeley: U of California P, 1982.

Sapir, Edward. *Culture, Language, and Personality*. Berkeley: U of California P, 1949.

Sidney, Sir Philip. *An Apology for Poetry*. *The Golden Hind*. Ed. Roy Lamson and Hallett Smith. New York: Norton, 1956. 271–309.

Stern, Arthur A. "When Is a Paragraph?" *The Writing Teacher's Sourcebook*. Ed. Gary Tate and E. P. J. Corbett. Oxford: Oxford UP, 1981. 294–300.

Strachey, James, ed. *The Complete Psychological Works of Sigmund Freud*. Vol. 5. London: Hogarth, 1964. 24 vols.

Vygotsky, Lev. *Thought and Language*. Trans. Eugenia Hanfmann and Gertrude Vaker. Cambridge: MIT P, 1962.

Winterowd, W. Ross. "Review of *The Prospect of Rhetoric*." *Philosophy and Rhetoric* 6 (1973): 47–59.

Wittgenstein, Ludwig. *Philosophical Investigations*. Trans. G. E. M. Anscombe. Oxford: Oxford UP, 1953.

Young, Richard, Alton Becker, and Kenneth Pike. *Rhetoric: Discovery and Change*. New York: Harcourt, 1970.